the river in my backyard

by Mikkel Aaland

THE RIVER IN MY BACKYARD

By Mikkel Aaland
Copyright © 2016 Mikkel Aaland. All rights reserved.

Cyberbohemia Press
San Francisco/Ulefoss, Norway
editor@cyberbohemia.com

Cover & Interior Design: Lori Barra
Cover Photographs: River photo copyright © Mikkel Aaland
Insert photo copyright © Aaland archives
Production: Peter Truskier, Premedia Systems, Inc.
Managing Editor: Rebecca Morgan
Video Production: Pete Vilotti
Logo Design: Bruce Yelaska

Library of Congress Cataloging-in-Publication Data

Aaland, Mikkel, 1952-
The River in My Backyard/written and with photographs by
Mikkel Aaland
p. cm.

ISBN 978-0-9972610-1-1
1. Memoir. 2. Aaland, Mikkel, 1952- 3. Mental illness. 4. Patricide.
5. Norway. 6. Pilgrimage—Mt. Kailash. 7. Livermore. 8. Photography. 9.
Shinto rituals. 10.epigenetics/ghost genes.

First Edition, 2nd printing
This is the trade softcover edition.
Also available in deluxe hardcover, eBook, and audio editions.

To Lynn Ferrin and Jacques Gauchey.

PART 1

Family is like a river.
What our ancestors do upstream
flows down to us and what we do
flows down to our children
and their children.
Some people call it family karma,
some call it ghost genes.
I call it the river in my backyard.

—*the author*

The river I call my life is about to burst from its banks and take a course through hell. The date is December 11, 2004, a Saturday. I am at my desk in my home office in San Francisco. An early morning light illuminates the dense forest of apartments around me. The phone rings; my mom's voice is trembling.

"Your father, he's not moving!"

I take a deep breath and will myself to stay calm. Dad is healthy. Maybe he's had a stroke or something unexpected but it will be ok. He has cheated death before. I can't imagine him dead and my mother doesn't say he is.

"Yes, of course I called 911," she says, her voice a little more focused now.

"I'm coming," I say, slamming the phone down and running down the narrow hallway of our apartment to the bedroom where my wife Rebecca is reading a book to our two young daughters.

"Something's happened to Dad, to *Bestefar*." I speak lightly for the girls' sake and use the Norwegian word for grandfather, meaning best father, what our girls call him. "Mom said he isn't moving." Rebecca hears the tension in my voice.

She says one word: "Go."

The Eidselva and our backyard.
Ulefoss, Norway.

On the 45-minute drive to my parents' home in Livermore I make several calls to the local police, hoping to find out which hospital my father is at. Being early on Saturday, there is little traffic, thankfully, because I am clearly distracted. My mother's line stays busy. The 911 dispatcher has no news. I can't imagine life without Dad. If he is on his deathbed I want to get there in time to be by his side and say goodbye.

When I turn the corner to my parents' suburban house, my heart skips a beat. There it is—the home of my childhood, wrapped in yellow police tape like a gigantic Christmas present from the devil himself. I stop and slam the car into park. Police and EMTs are everywhere. Instinctively I reach for my camera, sitting on the seat next to me. I can't get out of the car fast enough and I slip on some moldy yellow leaves that smell of late fall. I watch my mother rush past a policeman, trying to get to me. I see panic on her face, and then she is close. She grabs my arm.

"He's dead." And then she says the words I will never, can never, forget. "He's dead and the police think it's your brother. He left a note. They think Hans killed Dad."

I look past Mom, past the uniforms, past the yellow tape to the garage and see my father's partially naked body lying motionless on the floor just inside the door. I am a photographer, but taking a photograph now is the farthest thing from my mind. I struggle to breathe and try to push by a policeman to my father's side. He stiffens and stands firmly in my way. He's a homicide detective and he wants to know who I am. My mother answers for me.

"He's my oldest. He lives in San Francisco with his family."

The detective noticeably relaxes. I am not the son they are looking for.

"This is a crime scene," he says, pointing to the black letters on the yellow tape: POLICE LINE DO NOT CROSS. "Wait with your mother at the corner. We'll question you later."

I don't move. Seeing my father treated like a discarded slab of bloodless meat is too much. "At least cover him," I plead, waving my arms as though I could conjure some sort of barrier between my father's dead body and the group of curious neighbors and onlookers.

I shudder and tears fill my eyes.

The detective orders a black plastic sheet placed over my father, and my mom and I start toward the corner a few houses away. I turn my head back to the detective.

"There is no way my brother killed our father," I say with certainty. "He may be crazy, but he loves our father, just like I do."

The detective looks skeptical.

We aren't allowed near the house all day. Along with curious neighbors, we watch dazed from a distance as police officers come and go. I make calls from my cell phone to Rebecca, to friends, and to Nøve, my father's sister in Norway. I leave the cause of death unclear. I can't reach my middle brother, Erik, who is a longshoreman at the shipyard in Oakland. His phone is switched off.

The search for my brother Hans continues. The police are guarded and unhelpful. We are the victim's family, but in their eyes we are also related to the suspect.

Finally I reach Erik. It's his lunch break and he has turned on his cell phone.

"Erik, I've got bad news. Dad is dead."

At first he doesn't respond and I wonder if he heard me.

My brothers and I in Livermore
sitting on the couch our grandfather built,
next to our father's radio.

Then he replies with disbelief in his voice, "He was asleep when I left this morning."

Like our younger brother Hans, Erik still lives at home in Livermore.

"He is dead. I saw him. I am so sorry." It feels wrong to talk to him this way. I wish he were in front of me and I could hug him.

"Oh no! Oh no! " he cries, the reality hitting him. "How did he die? Was it a heart attack? What was it? How did he die?"

Pause. What should I say? "We aren't sure."

"Oh my god," he cries over and over. "Is there anything we could have done? Could we have saved him? "

"Erik," I say gently, "I don't think so, not this time. Come as quick as you can, ok? Mom needs us."

Just before I disconnect Erik asks, "Where is Hans? Is he there? Is he with Mom? Is he ok?"

I tell him the truth, but only part of it. "We don't know where he is. I'm sure he is ok."

Erik is silent for a moment then says he is on his way.

Now I am alone on the sidewalk on the corner. Mom is resting inside a neighbor's house. I know the corner of California and Estate well. As a child, over forty years ago, I crossed it every day on my way to kindergarten. When it rained the gutter always backed up and the street became a small suburban river. I wore yellow rain pants and a hooded jacket and black rubber boots and could splash happily through the ankle-deep water. I was protected. I was safe. I welcomed the rain and the overflow that covered the asphalt and transformed my street into something exotic and beautiful. That was then. There is no rain gear on earth that will protect me now. The water around me is deep and way over my head. I feel I am being sucked along with a torrent of water into the storm drain. I stand and watch the police come and go from the house I used to call home.

The carefree child that was me so many years ago had no clue what was waiting for him.

2

Later in the day I am still standing on the corner. I've made calls to everyone I know but I have barely moved. I haven't eaten and I am not hungry. As I snap photos of the yellow tape barricading the intersection, a police car pulls up to the curb. The same officer I spoke with earlier in the day leans out of the window of the patrol car and tells me the news.

"We arrested your brother. He was downtown. He didn't resist. He is in custody now." Then the officer reaches out the window and pulls down the tape blocking the entrance to California Way and drives away before I can ask anything.

Waiting on the corner I've had lots of time to think about everything, and now I am convinced the police are mistaken. Hans didn't do it. Dad died of natural causes, like a heart attack or a stroke. Even though he was in good health, he was 80 and he pushed himself. He flew back and forth between Livermore and Norway on a regular basis, and he maintained the lifestyle of a much younger person. I never imagined he would die in bed. But that must be what happened. His body simply gave out.

Why would my brother kill him? He had nothing to gain by killing Dad. He had issues with Dad—we all did—but nothing serious enough to lead to murder. Money? My parents live month to month off their small retirement checks. They've always been generous when Hans needed help. Attention? The murder would definitely give Hans attention, something he always craved. But there are lots of other ways to get attention. Twenty-five years to life is a lot to pay for the spotlight.

Why did he leave a note? Why did he say he did it? Easy; Hans is delusional. He must have seen Dad lying near his bed, dead, and said to himself, "Oh my god, look what happened. It must have been something I said or thought." That's Hans; the world is supposed to revolve around him, but that doesn't make him a murderer. He's a gentle, if a bit odd, 46-year-old man who loves riding his unicycle and works delivering pizza for a local restaurant.

Or is he?

For Thanksgiving just a few weeks ago, Hans was at our house with my parents, our brother Erik and Erik's girlfriend Bea. Thanksgiving is my favorite holiday. It is always a good excuse for family and friends to gather and eat without unreasonable expectations. I grilled a 23-pound free-range turkey on the Weber as usual. Its savory hickory smell filled the dining room. Everyone was hungry and jovial.

Hans sat rigidly at the table on my left, next to our father, expressionless while I proposed a toast. His finger was bloody and bandaged. He'd cut it earlier while slicing the traditional San Francisco crusty sourdough bread, and had nonchalantly dripped blood all over the kitchen floor. He made me nervous and I felt something had come over him. He was so wound up, like a guitar string stretched too tight.

I proceeded with the toast. I spoke about how earlier in the day my daughter Miranda wove a lovely scarf for her stuffed companion Beary, using just her fingers.

"Our family is like that," I continued. "It's a beautiful tapestry made from individual strings. And for that I am very thankful."

I raised my glass, which I had forgotten to fill.

"Hear, hear!" called Rebecca from the far end of the table.

Hans suddenly became animated. "Y.A.R. Y.A.R.," he cried, using his arms to spell out the letters of the acronym. "You. Are. Right.

"Mikkel made a toast and doesn't have any wine!" He reached quickly for the bottle of white and forcefully filled my glass. He was aggressive, like with the knife and the bread earlier. It scared me.

At the far end of the table I heard Mom repeat over and over, "I have something to say. I have something to say." Rebecca was sitting next to her, videotaping everything, and called for everyone to be quiet and listen to Beth. Rebecca can make herself heard when she wants to.

"One for all, and all for one!" Mom said, with a dramatic gesture toward the table filled with turkey, stuffing, mashed potatoes and other Thanksgiving trimmings. She was repeating another one of Hans' favorite sayings. I groaned quietly thinking that there was no need to encourage him.

Dad, who had been eyeing the food on his plate the whole time, let go of his home-made hearing aid—a customized Radio Shack intercom—that always hangs around his neck, and said softly, "All right, now we can drink." Dad liked to eat, but he knew we had to get through the toasting part first.

In the midst of all the competing voices I heard Erik propose, "Here's to chaos!" And because he always repeats himself to make sure he is heard in this family starved for attention, he

said it again. "Here's to chaos!" I heard him, and deep down I knew his was the most appropriate toast.

Back in the present with the police car long out of sight, Dad dead, and Hans sitting in a jail cell, I wonder whether I am the delusional one. Maybe Hans is guilty after all. If he is, chaos just became a full-fledged member of our family.

3

Near the end of this dreadful day they move my father's body. It is now dark and the flashing lights of the police cars reflect off the windows of the neighbors' parked cars and homes. The air is damp and the cold has become piercing. The awful yellow tape still encircles our front yard, making my childhood home a spectacle.

I try one last time to get close to my father as they move him, but an officer waves me off. I watch silently from the corner along with Mom, a few neighbors, and Erik, who arrived soon after I called him, as paramedics transfer my father's covered body to a stretcher and then to the quietly waiting ambulance.

Now what?

As a newspaper photographer, I have shot my share of car accidents, fires, and crime scenes. But it has always been someone else's drama, not mine. The distance between the story and me is gone. This is not work, but rather the most intimate of personal matters made public. Where can I go for comfort? I don't believe in a Christian heaven or hell, but I want to believe my father is still with us in some form. I place my hands together, bend my head forward, and pray. I want him to know I am here and that he isn't alone. It is all I can do for now.

Since the police won't let her back in the house, I convince my mother to stay with us in San Francisco, at least for the night. She puts up a tired resistance but finally agrees. Erik will stay with neighbors and keep an eye on the house.

On the drive back to San Francisco, Mom and I don't talk. Silence sits between us like a welcome guest, sensibly keeping us from sharing thoughts about Hans and the possibility of his guilt. Then, just past the Hayward-680 turnoff, twenty minutes from the city, Mom says very quietly, "Last night your father and I were up past midnight talking. He was with Hans in Pi Pi yesterday and they had come home late."

Pi Pi is the Miwok tribal name for the steep valley in the Sierra where my parents bought ten acres of forested land in the '60s. The wild Consumes River runs through the property. I haven't been there in years; I got tired of helping Dad with never-ending building projects that messed up the beautiful forest.

"Your father ate the cheesecake I baked him. He was tired and anxious. He talked about the properties in Norway, Livermore, and the buildings at Pi Pi that needed work. He said it was all getting to be too much for him to manage.

"Hans was with him. Your father said he walked around most of the day, staring up at the clouds. Dad asked Hans to help, but all Hans wanted to do was talk about the Bible, and you know how your father feels about that."

I did. Our father was a scientist, and lived very much in the rational world. He was from Norway, and very pragmatic. When he and Hans talked about the Bible or Jesus, it was like watching two trains going in opposite directions. There was never any physical confrontation between them, but when the conversation ended they were very far apart.

I listen carefully to my mom, waiting for some kind of revelation. I ask her gently, "Did he mention anything else that happened between him and Hans? Did they fight?"

My father as a young man in Norway, circa 1940.
Police tape across California Way, 2004. (Insert)

Mom adds after a long pause, "No. But he was really worried about Hans."

She stops, and then says more to herself than to me, "I really need to talk with your father again."

Just before we drive onto the Bay Bridge, one of our tires goes flat. I quickly pull as far as I can out of the heavy traffic and call roadside assistance. It's too dangerous to get out of the car. Vehicles speed by, dangerously close, and our car shakes as they pass.

There is nothing to do but wait for help to arrive. Suddenly my cell phone rings. It is Bruce Taylor, a long-time family friend who has been with us most of the day. His dad, also a scientist, worked at the Livermore Lab with my father, and was once mayor of Livermore. The Taylor family still has ties with many city officials.

"Are you ready for this?" Bruce asks.

I'm quiet. I can't imagine anything else going wrong.

"Your mom's house was just red-tagged," he says. "The police called the building inspector and when they came they found code violations. No one can go into the house without permission."

"My parents lived there for over 50 years!" I say, stunned. "And now of all days they find code violations?"

"There is nothing you can do," says Bruce. "I am here. I see red tags all over the house. Maybe on Monday we can do something and I can...."

My phone battery gives out after all the day's calls. No matter. I turn to my mom. She overheard our conversation.

"Mom? Are you ok?"

She doesn't answer. Her face is pale and drawn. In just a

few hours she has lost her husband, her home, and for all practical purposes, her youngest son. I can't imagine what is going through her head, or her heart.

I see her lips tighten; her eyes shut briefly and then open. Incredibly, she answers,

"I'll be alright."

A large tow truck arrives about fifteen minutes later and stops behind us. The driver uses a loudspeaker to tell me to drive forward, slowly, until I am out of the way of traffic. He will follow behind with bright flashing caution lights. After we park in a safe spot near the toll plaza, the tow truck drives away. I get out of the car and replace the flat tire with the spare. With my hands covered in dirt and grease, I drive across the bridge toward the sparkling lights of San Francisco. The panorama in front of me looks like a scenic postcard.

Suddenly, out of the blue, I imagine a horrible sequence of events. First I see my mother slumped in her seat, corpse-like, her heart shattered. As I watch from afar, I see Hans hanging from a belt tied to a cellblock window and Erik lying smashed under a tractor-trailer run amok. I see flames explode from the roof of the house in Livermore. In the time it takes for me to change lanes and exit into San Francisco, this nightmare fantasy has devastated me. It has taken what Hans started and completed the destruction.

Once we're home in North Beach my vision fades as quickly as it appeared. My daughters jump up and down, excited to see me. Rebecca stands in the narrow hallway watching me carefully, and then draws me into a long hug. I take a deep breath, drawing in the sweet smell of life. Rebecca turns and hugs my too-quiet mother. There is so much good left in the world.

After we prepare a bed for my mom and eat some canned

My daughters Ana and Miranda.

vegetable soup, I read to the girls in their room. After they are asleep, I go around the apartment carefully making sure all the windows are closed and the locks secure. We live in an Edwardian building built in 1913, but suddenly I wish we lived in a medieval fortress with a moat. I can't sleep. I get up and check on the girls, making sure they are ok. At one point, I climb into the top bunk with Miranda and engulf her protectively in my arms. After a while I do the same to Ana in the bottom bunk. I feel my family is under attack by a force I can only call evil. It's indiscernible, yet it has produced a caustic wave that has destroyed my father, my brother, my car tire, and my peace of mind. Just before dawn, I fall into a fitful sleep.

4

The date was April 21st, 1962. It was my father's 38th birthday, and arguably the coldest year of the Cold War. It was a Saturday in Livermore, and my father was very much alive. I was nine years old and I felt pretty good about myself. I spent a lot of time in front of the mirror combing my blond hair. I flexed my arm vainly to produce a small bulge in my biceps. I proudly wore the Norwegian sweater my grandmother knit me to school, and I enjoyed my oily sardine sandwich, despite the looks of disgust from my friends. I hadn't reached the age yet when I wore dorky glasses and felt embarrassed about my Norwegian otherness and ungainly limbs. I was a child, and I still thought my father could do no wrong and that my mother was a saint.

My six-year-old brother Erik and I were in the living room of our house on California Way, watching *Captain Kangaroo*— or was it *Sky King*?—in black and white. Hans, who was three, was with our mom. I don't remember what they were doing, but I do remember neither of them was involved in what happened next.

Erik and I heard a Snap! Bang! and then a voice crying for help from the front yard. Even now I can still hear his voice clearly. At first we weren't sure who was in trouble. It took a moment to connect the distressed voice to my father.

We rushed outside to see Dad pinned underneath a huge, heavy plate of corrugated metal. It was the floor section from a Southern Pacific boxcar that our father was using to build a bomb shelter. Dad moved his head from side to side, moaning in pain. His steel-framed glasses were smashed and twisted on his grimacing face. He was a big man, a little thick around the middle, but solid and very strong. Still, the weight was slowly crushing the life out of him.

At first Erik and I just stared. Our father was in mortal danger, but we were just kids. What could we do? Lying next to Dad was the broken and now useless winch he was using to lift the heavy plate. It was wedged under the plate and kept thousands of pounds of metal from flattening Dad completely like a pancake.

We looked at the winch, then questioningly at each other. Without a word we stood on either side of Dad and gripped the cold edge of the plate and lifted. Miraculously the plate budged and our father squirmed his way out from underneath.

Once he was safe, Erik and I dropped the plate and the winch shattered with a loud crunch. We couldn't believe what we just did. We didn't know anything about adrenaline; we just knew we did something impossible with our backs and our small bare hands and the love we shared for our father.

Our father was lucky. No bones were cracked, and he spent only a few days on the couch waiting for his sprained back

My father and the bombshelter (insert).

to heal. Erik and I were unbelievably proud of what we were able to do. We saved our father's life! He was thankful, of course, but he was never overly emotional. I sensed he took what we did for granted. He would do anything for us, so why wouldn't we do the same for him? I ultimately felt let down. I was hungry for more acknowledgment.

Soon Dad was his usual active self, going to work at the Livermore Radiation Laboratory—the Lab, as everyone called it—and coming home precisely at 5:00 p.m. He ate, then donned his Big Ben overalls, the ones with the gray herringbones, and resumed work on the bomb shelter.

He was obsessed with the shelter. He wanted to protect us. The idea of an all-out nuclear war with the Soviet Union was not so far fetched in 1962. Dad knew that the Lab, where nuclear weapons research took place, was a certain target for a Soviet nuclear warhead. He'd been to underground tests in Nevada, and knew the power of nuclear explosions. I was only nine. I didn't yet understand how his fears were seeping into me, becoming mine.

"The best offense," he said, "is a good defense." He told us this with a heavy Norwegian accent. I couldn't hear the accent. I only knew he had one because the kids on the block teased me about it.

Thanks to Erik and me, Dad was still in one piece, and went on to finish constructing the bomb shelter in October. The Cuban Missile Crisis blew over in November and the U.S. and the Soviet Union avoided a nuclear war. Eventually, the bomb shelter became my bedroom and protected me in other ways. But I am getting ahead of myself.

On that day back in 1962 I learned a valuable lesson. For a brief moment I became powerful beyond my wildest imagination. I saw what I could do if I had to. Now, so many years later, I wish I could use that power again to save my father.

Alas, no matter what you wish for, you can never step into the same river twice.

5

Early the day after my father's death, I pace the oil-stained floor of the Big O Tire garage as the mechanic repairs the Saab's punctured tire. I am in a hurry; I have so many things to do. What's taking him so long? Once the tire is fixed I start the hour-long drive back to Livermore.

I cross the Bay Bridge, which my daughters call the "Grandma Bridge" because both of their grandmothers live on the other side, my mom in Livermore and Rebecca's mom in Berkeley. As I settle into the familiar drive, I am calmer than I was yesterday, but that is not saying much. I follow Interstate 580 through Oakland, Hayward, and finally over the oak and grass-covered hills to Pleasanton and Livermore. The hills have so far been spared suburban sprawl, and today the yellow parched grass is just starting to show a hint of green. Winter is coming.

Livermore, my hometown, lies in the center of the valley. It has grown a lot since I left for college in 1970, and is struggling to keep its small-town charm. The only reason I go back now is to visit my parents. I remember two roadside signs that were torn down years ago, but will always remain for me. One sign welcomed visitors to Livermore, the Atomic City. The other announced the annual Livermore Rodeo in mid-June, "the fastest rodeo in the world." Scientists and cowboys. This is the Livermore I remember, even with the signs gone.

At one time Livermore boasted the second-highest number of Ph.D.'s per capita in the country, just behind Los Alamos, another nuclear weapons research facility. Half my friends' parents were physicists. The other half were ranchers. People of the earth and people of the mind. I can't imagine two groups with so little in common, and yet we all managed to get along, by and large.

I drive through downtown Livermore to East Avenue, the long street that dead-ends at the Lab after passing my parents' home. The Lab sits on the site of a former Naval Air Force base, a collection of high-security buildings spread over a full square mile. It was built in 1952, the year I was born. In 1955 my father, a U.C. Berkeley-trained electrical engineer and a recent immigrant from Norway, was hired by the Lab to work on magnetic triggering devices for nuclear bombs. Other fathers drove cars or rode bikes up this long wide street to work. My father, dressed in a white shirt and tie, often commuted on roller skis, even though there was never any snow. I never thought of my father as graceful, but when he poled and kicked and glided to work or skied in the mountains, his movements were light and efficient, and he moved quickly and smoothly.

Long before reaching the Lab, I turn left from East Avenue onto Estate Street, which used to be called Atomic Street in the 1950s. I pass Harvard Way and then Princeton Way before turning right onto California Way. There are no crowds of police around the house this morning, and the street is quiet. Many of the neighbors are at church. The yellow crime scene tape is gone, replaced by red-tag notices stapled to the walls and doors of my parents' home, warning that no one may enter.

I rip one of the notices from the wall and go directly to the guest bedroom in the garage where my father occasionally slept and where he died. Sheets and blankets from Dad's bed lie haphazardly on the floor. Briefly I envision him as I saw him yesterday, lifeless, and wearing only his underwear, sprawled awkwardly on the concrete floor. Suddenly I sense something. It's him—I know it instantly. A part of him is hovering over the spot where his body lay.

My father didn't expect to die yesterday. Healthy at 80, he clearly had good years left in him. He looked forward to spending them with his grandchildren and the crazy projects he loved so much. He was very stubborn and I can easily imagine him not accepting his own death.

I yell into the room, "You are dead, Dad!"

He had been hard of hearing in life, so I yell it several times, each louder than before. "DAD! YOU ARE DEAD!"

As my words echo around the room, I feel a change. My father's presence is still strong, but now I can imagine a confused look on his face. He has heard me, but he is not sure what to do. Then I get the distinct feeling my father understands what I am telling him. He knows he is dead. He knows what to do. I feel his presence dissolve with an upward motion and a whoosh. I feel an immediate sense of relief that I am now alone in the room.

I grip the red-tag notice in my hand and crumple it up. Tossing it on the ground, I lock up and head back to my car. My father has moved on, and so must I.

My final stop is the Livermore Police Station to check on my brother Hans. He is not there. They have transferred him to the nearby Santa Rita county jail, and he's on suicide watch. One of the officers I recognize from yesterday steps into the lobby and I have a brief conversation with him. He is sympathetic, but when I express doubt about Hans' guilt, he recounts disturbing details that I haven't heard before. There is the note, and Hans' statement to both neighbors and the police, but also, the police also found Dad's wallet in Hans' room along with a t-shirt Hans said he used to suffocate

Dad. All the evidence adds up. There is no question about it: Hans planned and then murdered our father in cold blood. It was easy for me to say I loved my brother when I wasn't sure what had happened. Now I am pissed. He is a murderer and that changes everything.

6

On Monday morning, on my way to Café Trieste for my morning coffee, I pick up a copy of the *San Francisco Chronicle*. A headline screams at me:

> *Eccentric accused of killing his father. Victim, 80, was former scientist at weapons lab.*

The sensationalized article, read by hundreds of thousands of other readers all over northern California, continues:

> *Hans Aaland has for years been Livermore's living oddity—riding a 12-foot-tall unicycle in a jester hat, passing out protest leaflets, addressing the City Council on the "beauty of the community," and spouting revelations from God.*

> *The 46-year-old man had a few run-ins with the law as well, but some people who know him say they were shocked nonetheless by his arrest this weekend on suspicion of killing his father.*

> *Police say Aaland smothered his father, Kristian Aaland, early Saturday as the father slept in the bedroom of the home he shared with his son and wife. Hans Aaland, police said, told his mother what he had done, left a confession note full of biblical quotations and walked away from the home.*

> *Next-door neighbor Dan Emmrich said he knew Hans Aaland wasn't like everyone else but, "I never thought he was dangerous.*

Kristian Aaland, 80, an eccentric former scientist at the Lawrence Livermore National Laboratory who buried a boxcar in his front yard as a bomb shelter during the Cold War, was found dead at 10:30 a.m. Saturday after his wife called for help, said police Sgt. Jim Suibielski.

Police entering the home on the 3900 block of California Way were so stunned by the conditions inside that they summoned building inspectors, who that same day red-tagged the building. Suibielski said some of the oddities included bare electrical wires, crudely built additions and stairwells, the bomb shelter, and stacks of belongings piled everywhere.

"The house is just incredible," Suibielski said. "It is not capable of human occupancy."

At this point in the article I toss the paper down in disgust and several of the café patrons look at me, startled. I feel both humiliated and furious. Even though I know Suibielski is out of line, even though I know my friends will read the article and know better, I still want to run and hide. They have turned my family, including me, into circus freaks, something to put on a reality TV show. Oh my God. What about my mother? She's lived in Livermore for over 50 years. She was a special ed teacher, respected by students and parents alike, and a tireless community activist. Will people remember that, or will they remember this goddamn newspaper article? It's easy to say Screw them, but it hurts and tears me up inside.

Later that day, across the street from the Little City Market, I run into one of my daughter's classmates walking home from school with his father. The boy asks me politely if my brother used a gun, holding his hand up in a pistol grip as he talks. His father is clearly embarrassed and whisks his son away with an apology before I can answer.

Rebecca and I have to tell our daughters about what Hans,

their crazy uncle, has done. There is no way to hide the truth, even though we want to.

We seek expert advice, and are counseled to tell the girls the truth, but not to give too many details unless or until they specifically ask for them. Most important, the girls must feel safe. They need to know Rebecca and I are safe, too, and that Hans is not a threat now. I do not want them to feel that what their uncle did is a reflection on them. We tell them that *Bestefar* is dead because of Uncle Hans, who is sick, and that Hans' illness made him do it.

Of course they have questions. Miranda, who is nine, is reticent about asking for specific details, but listens carefully when I answer her five-year-old sister's questions. Ana wants to know exactly how her grandfather, *Bestefar*, died. We tell her Uncle Hans put a pillow over his head. Somehow, to us, a pillow seems less threatening than any other means of suffocation.

"Pillow?" she repeats. "I put a pillow over my head and I don't die."

More questions follow. "Why couldn't we see Uncle Hans doing it?" she asks. "If we had, we could have stopped him."

I try to reassure her that she is safe and that Hans is confused and sick—that he thought he was helping *Bestefar*. "He didn't want to die, did he?" she asks. Her best friend's great-grandmother has just died at 100. "Why couldn't *Bestefar* live that long?" she asks.

She also doesn't get the part about Hans being sick. "When I'm sick," she says, "I don't get confused." I explain it is a sickness of the mind but she doesn't understand.

"What is the difference?" she asks, but I can't think of a good answer.

The entire time she is asking questions, I feel as though I am walking on a river of thin ice. I try to be light and gentle, and not show just how scared and upset I really am.

7

When I wake up on Tuesday morning,

it's cold and rainy. Finally the weather matches my mood. I take the girls to school, then slip back into bed fully dressed and pull the covers over my head. Rebecca is upstairs with my mother. We encouraged her to stay with us until after the Christmas holidays, when, if she wants, she can find a new place in Livermore.

My respite under the sheets doesn't last long.

Rebecca appears and starts folding clothes on the bed, on top of me. She is obviously upset.

"What is wrong?' I ask, annoyed.

"Your mom! I can't believe what she just said."

"What?"

"She said Hans is not mentally ill. She defended him!"

I sit up. "She defended him against murder? I don't believe it."

Rebecca tosses a single sock on the bed. "No, no. Not against murder. She said Hans is not mentally ill."

I pause, then say, "Mom doesn't like labels, she never did."

"But this has been the problem all along!" cries Rebecca. "She doesn't face reality. It was obvious he needed help."

"We all tried," I say wearily. "We all tried, for a long time."

"I'm not so sure," says Rebecca. "It's not normal for a 46-year-old man to live at home, not normal to hear voices and see Jesus' face on mountains."

"I know my family isn't perfect, but I never imagined it falling apart like this. I am so sorry."

Rebecca moves away from the bed and sits on a nearby chair. "I love your mom and I really miss your dad. It's painful to see your family, our family, like this."

She drops her head momentarily and then looks up and adds, "My side of the family has issues too."

"Yeah, but no one has killed anyone." I sigh. "Now let me rest, please. I promise to get up and help in a little while."

I'm not in bed long. Beyond the daily household chores there is so much to do. Rebecca and I, my mother, and Erik all agree it is best to hold the memorial service as soon as possible, before Christmas. We settle on Sunday, December 19th. We will all benefit from the warm embrace of our caring community of friends and family, which has already shown support by delivering ready-made meals to our doorstep.

Getting the word out about the ceremony is easy. Because of the media attention, almost everyone already knows about my father's death. We receive a stream of callers who offer condolences and welcome the news of the upcoming memorial service. We aren't the only ones shaken by the event and in need of comfort.

There are so many other things to deal with. My father was scheduled to fly back to Norway in a week, so I call the travel agent to cancel his ticket and request a refund.

"You want to know why he isn't going?" I ask the agent, fully aware of the rigid guidelines for a refund. "He's dead. Is that a good enough reason?"

At first there is only silence on the line. Then, "Let me check." After a minute or so she says, "Ok, but the taxes are not refundable."

I consider making a comment about death and taxes, but don't. My sense of humor, limited as it is, is missing.

All the while we find ourselves fielding phone calls from both the District Attorney's office and the Public Defender's office. One refers to us as family of the victim; the other office calls us family of the accused. It's all so confusing. Over time it becomes clear that Hans is very fortunate. He has a top-notch Public Defender assigned to him, and a District Attorney who seems very reasonable and who understands that Hans is mentally incompetent.

Then there is my father's body, the body I last saw wheeled away on a gurney.

I want to see him before he is cremated so that I can give him a proper goodbye. After a thorough autopsy by the Alameda County Coroner, the body is finally released to the Callaghan Mortuary in Livermore.

The mortuary is located on East Avenue, the same road that leads to the Lab. I used to walk by it every day on my way to school. It is the first place I saw a dead body. In 1966, my friend and classmate Randy Hewitt died of brain cancer. His embalmed remains lay in state at Callaghan's for everyone to pay their respects to. Randy was dressed in a tan suit, and his handsome face was so peaceful, yet so plastic looking. Even though I had reservations about seeing him dead, I was glad I did. It made his death real and final, which was strangely comforting for my teenage self, still unaccustomed to death. It helped prepare me for today.

It is Saturday, the day before the ceremony. I'm with my close friend Tom Mogensen, who has come along for moral support. They tell us my father is in a back room, and they wave us in the general direction. The first room we enter is wrong. Lying on a gurney is the body of an elderly woman. We look at each other and shake our heads. It's an awkward moment, but it momentarily lessens my anxiety.

We quickly try the room next door.

After a brief hesitation, I go to my father's supine body. A sheet covers him up to his neck. I look at his pale face. His eyes and mouth are tightly closed. He appears flat and two-dimensional, devoid of character. Tom stands by the wall and quietly watches as I reach under the sheet and find my father's right hand. I clasp it. It is cold. I sense that Tom is worried about me. He doesn't know how I might react to seeing my father this way, but I am ok. I am finally with Dad.

His fingers are strong and calloused. They have gripped chainsaws, power drills, ski poles, saws, as well as gently holding me when I was young. His palm and knuckles are marred with deep cuts and sores. He rarely wore gloves. He cleaned his greasy hands with gasoline and I can vividly remember the powerful smell. I also remember him finishing up with a bar of Lava soap, a coarse soap made from pumice, and sometimes with steel wool.

I look at Dad's neck for signs of my brother's hands. Seeing nothing, I remember the police said Hans used a t-shirt to suffocate him. I pull back the sheet and the skin below Dad's shirt line is as white as fresh snow. He burned easily in the sun; consequently he always protected himself from the harmful UV rays. What's missing is my father's distinct and comforting musky smell. He never smoked, but he was always around wood fires. The smell left with his spirit.

I reach for his mouth. I want to know if his teeth are intact. The morning he died I dreamed all my teeth had shattered. The dream was so real I carefully checked my mouth and made sure everything was ok before getting up and eating

*Frozen grass on the banks of the Eidselva,
Ulefoss, Norway.*

breakfast. Was there a connection between my dream and my father's death? I give Dad's jaw a half-hearted tug. It doesn't move and I stop trying. What difference does it make if his teeth are broken or not? He is dead.

By now I am sobbing and Tom pulls me gently away from my father and leads me out of the room. The next time I see my father, he is ash, divided into two shoebox-sized boxes. I can hardly believe this is all that is left of him. He was so large in life, yet now in death I can easily carry him in one hand.

8

Later that evening, after returning to San Francisco from the mortuary, I go to Tosca, a quiet neighborhood bar near Chinatown, next to North Beach. It is only a few days before Christmas and there aren't many people out, even though it is a Saturday. The historic City Lights bookstore across the street is nearly empty of customers. It's raining heavily and the wet streets reflect the multi-colored neon lights outside. I order an Anchor Steam beer and scribble notes on a napkin. I'm composing a eulogy for my dad, which I'll need to read tomorrow at his memorial service. I drink, then write. Drink. Write. What a day. Drink.

The memories flow smoothly. I write what I remember.

> *He welded steel roots and branches onto a long metal trunk and planted the "tree" in our backyard for us to build forts on. He angled a railroad spike through my car door to fasten it shut. He crafted a beautiful briefcase for me from wood, but it was so heavy I could barely carry it to school. How grateful I was when he hitchhiked from Livermore to meet the family at Samuel P. Taylor campground carrying my cat, Boots. When he custom made a three-person bicycle for my brothers and me that we rode all the time until Hans grew too big to fit in the pedal-less middle seat.*

After filling both sides of the napkin with notes, I write:

I love you Dad. I just want to hold your hand. I miss you. But now your hands are everywhere and I feel them.

I order one last beer then walk slowly home through the cold rain.

Just before the service on Sunday, the rain stops and it is bright, clear, and chilly. Callaghan's is quickly packed with over 100 friends and colleagues of my dad and mom. My cousin Jon Anders, who flew in from Norway with his oldest brother Bjørn Gregert, leads off with a hauntingly beautiful Norwegian folk song. Although I'm still dazed by my father's death and the beer from the evening before, the sound of my cousin's voice brings the mountains, trees, and rivers of Norway, and therefore my father, into sharp focus. I read the eulogy I wrote the night before. Many others then stand up and do likewise, sharing memories of the bomb shelter, Dad roller skiing to work; his accomplishments at the Lab; his love of building; and his obsession with Citroëns, the French cars he drove and regularly had to repair.

My childhood friend Steve Bloxham remembered my father's pragmatic side.

"I showed up at your house and your dad was furious," Steve says, looking at me as he speaks. "He couldn't find a single matching sock. He left and came back a short while later with a box full of black socks: 100 pairs of them!"

Rebecca's mother Francisca is there, sitting with her husband Steve and Rebecca's brother Michael. She is a Spanish beauty who once caught the fancy of the actor Marlon Brando when he met her at a party in southern California. According to family lore, Brando walked into the room, saw the lovely young Francisca and marched over and planted a kiss on her lips. Francisca always blushes when someone tells this story.

*The metal tree my father
built in our backyard.
Livermore, circa 1963.*

More important to me, she is a librarian at the Berkeley Public Library. I've always had a soft spot for these noble keepers of books, ever since 6th grade when the East Avenue School librarian fed me a nourishing diet of Heinlein, Asimov, and Bradbury,

Francisca gets up and recalls an intimate moment during Rebecca's and my wedding when she and my dad shared memories of their move to the States, she from Franco's Spain, and Dad from the recently liberated Norway.

"We had a lot in common," she says, wiping her eyes with her handkerchief. "We both felt caught between two different worlds."

She doesn't talk about it now, but there is another reason my father's death is particularly painful for her. During the Spanish Civil War, partisans assassinated her father. She was only a nine-month-old baby, and the trauma seeped into her bones and left her emotionally vulnerable. Sadly, almost four years later to the day, we will lose Francisca to another tragic, terrible event.

Hans is the elephant in the room. Even though almost all of the people in the room know him, many from childhood, he is not mentioned once during the service. A few people come up to me afterwards and privately tell me how much they always liked Hans, and how they can't understand why he did what he did. He was a popular student in high school, and always the center of attention. He was on the track team and was often the lead in school plays and musicals.

"It is so sad," says one of our old neighbors who used to babysit Hans. "So sad."

Then a family friend whispers in my ear, "How did you turn out so normal?"

She means this is a compliment, but I don't take it that way.

She doesn't know me that well.

"Thank you," I say, and let the conversation end there.

Even though the service is a soothing salve, it is only goes skin deep. Under the surface I feel beaten up. Will I feel this broken the rest of my life? When we asked the grief counselor how to tell our girls about what Hans did, he singled me out for special advice. He was worried about me.

"There are predictable steps in the grieving process," he explained. "You are in shock now. Expect anger, sadness, and then eventually acceptance to follow. Everyone reacts a little differently, but ultimately time heals all."

It sounded good. I wish I could just let go and let time do its thing. But it's not that simple. People lose their parents all the time, but my father didn't just die. He was murdered by my brother. I am not only grieving the death of my father, but the collapse of my family. I would love a detailed, ready-made map to guide me through the twists and turns and barriers that now lie between me and happiness. Or better yet, I wish there were a magic wand I could wave and make everything whole again. I feel if I don't do something, things are only going to get worse.

Life is so much harder now.

9

Typically I start getting depressed the moment I hear a Christmas song on the radio or see the first Christmas ad in the paper. Maybe it has something to do with not getting my expectations met as a child at this time of year. Maybe I just don't like the winter darkness, or the hypocrisy I see all around me. There is just something about the season that gets me down. For obvious reasons, this Christmas is worse than ever. It's hard to be joyful, and it doesn't help when you have two young children who love Christmas and call you the Grinch.

At least the winter solstice, December 21st, is past. The shortest day of the year is over. The darkness starts to recede and the days start to get longer. Even though the change is barely noticeable, just the thought of more light makes me feel better.

Our mailbox is filled with Christmas cards and condolences. It is a strange mix of messages, and they push and pull me in different directions. One card is cheerful and full of hope for the coming year. The next is dark and serious. "So sorry for your loss." The words "tragic" and "shocking" are not used, but they are always there as subtext.

In the middle of all this I get a troubling email from my Japanese friend Kazz Tagami. His response to my email telling him about my father's death is neither cheerful Christmas greeting nor sympathetic condolence.

"You and your family are in danger," he writes. "You have to be very careful."

I know Kazz well, yet he always surprises me. He is not typically Japanese; for that matter, he isn't typical in any way. He lives alone and operates a small rice farm near Osaka, and collects and sells antiques during the winter. He is also a practicing Shintoist, and spends his free time praying and studying the old Shinto ways. I've known Kazz since the early '80s, and in 1994 he met my family at Rebecca's and my wedding in St. Helena in the Napa Valley. He officiated in his capacity as a Shinto priest and even got our parents to make offerings to the sun goddess during the ceremony, even though none of us are Shintoists. He is my age, but often acts as my spiritual guide.

"Bad spirits have taken control of your brother," he continues. "They are probably low animal spirits who just want to make trouble for humans. Be careful. They will try and trick you."

If you don't know Kazz or his Shinto belief system like I do, his warning would seem very... well, strange. Spirits are part of everyday life for Kazz; as a Shintoist, he worships nature, and believes spirits of all kinds dwell in rocks, trees, and even rainbows. Shinto is an earth-based approach to spirituality, infused with magic and ritual aimed at bringing balance to everyday life.

When I first met Kazz, the world was severely out of balance and bad spirits engulfed the world. It was during the Cold War, and he and his *sensei*, and a group of survivors of Hiroshima, were battling the bad spirits in order to save the world from nuclear destruction. I had been deeply touched by their story and felt a connection, given my childhood in the bomb shelter. I spent much of the next six years trying to understand their point of view and trying to help bring balance back to the world. In the process, I learned a great deal about myself and my own inner demons.

Now, years later, Kazz claims bad spirits played a role in killing my father.

"The spirits who possessed your brother amplified even the smallest negative feelings he had towards your father," he writes. "They tricked him into believing his actions would save the world. You know from your time here in Japan that spirits are always trying to contact us. The highest spirit does it with no fanfare, and only produces good. But in this case lower spirits caused evil."

I take his warning seriously. Well, half seriously. Kazz and I are from two very different cultures and even though we have been through a lot together, I still find some of his beliefs hard to swallow. When I take what he says literally, my rational mind balks. After all, I am the son of a scientist. Bad spirits? Sure, right. But another part of me finds the idea of an outside factor strangely comforting. It helps me accept the irrationality of what happened.

Kazz isn't done with his warnings. What he writes next really hits a nerve.

"The murder of a parent by a child is one of the worst crimes of all. From a spiritual way of looking, your brother's crime is your family's crime."

Years ago, when I visited him at his home, Kazz compared the family to a river. "Everyone has his or her own family river," he explained. "Everything your ancestors do upstream, good and bad, flows downstream to all of us who follow. Even a small drop of bad upstream, like a toxin, can intensify and have far-reaching consequences downstream for succeeding generations."

"Sounds like karma," I replied as I struggled to understand exactly what he meant.

"Yes," he said, "but family karma. You are not only living your life for yourself, but for your children, and your children's children." It was then he also told me, "All evil in the world comes when ancestors are not shown proper respect."

With the image in my mind of a river connecting the past, the present, and the future, and binding the dead with the living, Kazz's final words in his email make perfect sense. "You have to make the river clean, and not leave the job up to the next generation, your daughters."

Instinctively I know he is right. This is what I have been feeling since Dad's death. Hans' act has contaminated us all, and I need to do something. I can't change what happened, but I can take responsibility for what comes next. It is only fair to my two young daughters and all who follow me. But the question is: how do I clean my family's river? How do I protect my daughters?

For now, Kazz does not provide an answer and I am on my own.

1 0

The bells of nearby St Peter and Paul

church chime happily on Christmas day. Inside our apartment Miranda and Ana rip through the presents under the Christmas tree. I make my traditional Norwegian heart-shaped waffles for breakfast. We cover the waffles with fresh whipped cream and the last of the amazing raspberry jam my father brought us from Norway. From now on we'll have to fetch the jam ourselves.

Rebecca runs around cleaning up after everyone. She is not happy about this. She thinks I let the girls get away with too much, and she is probably right. When I was growing up, our parents always told us not to have high expectations. They always said, "Money is tight," even though there was always enough to fund Dad's ambitious building projects. I don't want my girls to feel the same disappointment I did at Christmas. My mom reads the girls stories she has written for them. On the surface things look normal, but I'm using all the energy I have left to help make things appear that way.

On the day after Christmas, a powerful 9.2 earthquake strikes in the Indian Ocean, on the opposite side of the world. The entire planet vibrates and Rebecca and I see images of the huge tsunami wash ashore and kill more than 230,000 people. It is hell incarnate. Beaches in Thailand, Sri Lanka, and Bangladesh are littered with downed trees, smashed homes, and tangled bodies.

I turn from the horrific images on the TV to Rebecca, "This is exactly how I feel inside. Torn and broken." She nods. I know she feels the same way. But then she adds thoughtfully, "You know, there are always people who have it worse than we do."

It provides small comfort, but it is a thought I need to remember.

We quietly acknowledge New Year's Eve and say goodbye and good riddance to 2004. It's a year I want to quickly forget. The waters that have washed so violently over me are starting to recede back to their banks. The course of my life has perceptibly changed. I am on a new path and going in a direction I am not fully prepared for.

It starts with my parents' will. In an amendment, my father has followed tradition and left all his property in Norway to me, his oldest son. It is one of my favorite places on Earth, and I *should* be thrilled to inherit it.

The property includes a small piece of land with three buildings that have been in the family since 1893, plus a simple wood cabin on a small lake nearby. It is located in Ulefoss, a small town in Telemark, which is one of the most beautiful regions in the south of Norway. In the backyard of the family property is a real, not just metaphorical, river. Collectively the river is known as the Telemark Canal, but the section that flows through Ulefoss is called the Eidselva. Sections of the river are swift and turbulent but the part in our backyard flows slowly, bounded upstream and downstream with hydroelectric dams and locks that enable river boats and logs to pass safely through the turbulent falls. It sounds great, but to get there from San Francisco requires a long, expensive journey by plane over the Arctic Circle.

Dad left me an inheritance, filled with potential, but with no easy means to enjoy it.

To make things worse, my father left the property a mess. I know this because I had just been in Norway the fall before he died. I stopped there on my way to the Photokina conference in Germany to see my aunt Nøve, my dad's sister, who had just been diagnosed with cancer. I was only in Ulefoss a couple of days, but it was enough to see that things had gotten out of control. Citroëns and Citroën parts were strewn all over the garden and filled two of the three buildings. The only place left unaffected was the main house, occupied by two renters.

"I want to keep the property," I say to Rebecca, after reading the will. "But I think we should sell it. It's too far away, and too much for us to manage. Maybe one of my cousins will take it."

I don't even consider bringing in my brother Erik to help. Right now he has his hands full helping Mom in Livermore and anyway, after our mom passes, he will inherit Pi Pi. He will have his own mess to clean up then.

"We can't sell it! It's been in your family for so long," argues Rebecca, who has visited Norway with me several times. "The girls and I love it there. It's beautiful."

"But you haven't seen what I saw," I say. "Dad was out of control. He parked one of the old Citroëns on the strip between the workshop and the river. I have no idea how he even got it there! How are we are going to remove it? And what about everything else?"

After a few moments Rebecca replies thoughtfully, "Well, in any case you can't sell the property until we clean it up. Let's just take it step by step and play it by ear."

It was mid-May, 1962, just a month after Erik and I pulled Dad to safety from under the iron plate. The boxcar shell was now fully assembled and partially buried under tons of concrete and dirt. There was still a lot of work to do and Dad was in a hurry to finish. The Cuban Missile Crisis was not yet on the public radar but Dad believed the Soviet Union and the U.S. were clearly moving toward a confrontation. He didn't give us details, but we could understand why he was concerned. The Lab had accelerated its nuclear weapons development. Nearly every week Dad, along with a group of other scientists, flew to a top secret Nevada site for tests.

Mom and Dad decided to send Erik and me to Norway for the summer to keep us safe. To us, our front yard was a muddy playground, but in reality it was a dangerous construction zone. With summer break and lots of free time, we were bound to break a bone or cut ourselves on the many sharp objects strewn around.

"Hans will stay with us," our mother explained. He was only three years old, and my mom wasn't ready to let him go so young. I didn't think she was completely happy with the idea of us leaving. Dad, on the other hand, wanted us to spend time with his parents, and get to know where he grew up. In Norway I would also see first-hand the origins of his deep-seated fears and gain a better understanding of why the bomb shelter was so important to him.

On May 21st Erik and I boarded a plane for New York. Dad accompanied us on this first leg of the journey. In New York he helped us transfer to an Icelandic Airlines plane bound for Oslo via Reykjavik. He patted us on the shoulder and said goodbye. There were no hugs or kisses, no "I love you." I knew my dad by then, and I took his unsentimental departure for granted. We were on a grand adventure.

When we finally landed at Oslo's Fornebu airport, our grandfather and aunt were waiting for us on the tarmac. I recognized *Tante* Nøve at once. A year earlier she had visited us in Livermore and bought me my first camera, an Agfa Silette 35mm rangefinder with a real leather case. I had it hanging from my shoulder when she greeted me with a generous hug. I was disappointed to hear she was now living in Oslo with her boyfriend. She would accompany us to Ulefoss, but then visit only when her new job with an architectural firm allowed it.

This was the first time I met my grandfather, my *Bestafar*. I knew he made and sold furniture, but he didn't look at all like I had imagined him. Instead of an artisan with a thick white beard and rough country clothes, he was dressed in a suit and tie and looked like a businessman. He held his hat in both hands, smiling, while he nodded in greeting. Instinctively I knew a hug was out of the question, so I settled for a vigorous handshake. I was too young for metaphors, but I already sensed the family river at work: like father, like son.

It was a three-hour drive south from Oslo to Ulefoss on a narrow, windy country road. I fought jetlag and carsickness the whole way. When we finally pulled up into the gravel courtyard of the Aaland property, I was desperate to escape from the backseat of the tiny, two-door West German car. Nøve, however, had a few things to say first.

Pointing to the white, modest two-story house at one end of the small courtyard she said, "Your great-grandfather, Kristian Mikkelsen, built it in 1893. You were named after him and so was your father." And then she added, "Your father and I were both born in this house, as was your grandfather and his two sisters, your great-aunts."

After turning our attention toward a long, narrow building

Tante Nøve holding Hans with Mom in the background. Livermore, circa 1960.

adjacent to the house, she continued. "That is your grandfather's store, the *lager*." Above the store front windows were large wood block letters spelling out *H.K. Aaland Møbler* (furniture). "And that is where the furniture is crafted, the *verksted*," she said, gesturing toward a barn-like structure at the other end of the courtyard.

Our grandfather, who didn't understand or speak English, had been sitting quietly the whole time in the driver's seat. Now he spoke to Nøve in Norwegian, and it was our turn not to understand.

"Enough talk!" said Nøve laughing as she tossed her thick blond hair to the side and swung open the car door. "*Bestafar* says to let you out."

Just then our grandmother and grandfather's sister appeared at the porch of the main house. They hurried across the courtyard to greet us and help us out of the car. *Bestemor*, "best mother," and *Tante* Ingeborg were familiar faces. Both of them had spent extended time in Livermore helping raise us. They were dressed in traditional, hand-embroidered Norwegian *bunads*, the national costume used for special occasions, including welcoming visitors from America.

While *Bestafar* unloaded the car, the women guided us into the house. The first thing I noticed was the delicious odors of cinnamon and cardamom and the lingering smell of burnt firewood. On the oak table in the dining room were stacks of waffles, rolls of *krumkaker*, piles of *lefse*, and other delicious, home-baked treats. *Bestemor* and *Tante* Ingeborg beamed as Erik and I came to life, stuffing ourselves with the Norwegian specialties they had worked so hard to make.

Revived, we excused ourselves and bolted from the house back out to the courtyard. The river! Dad had talked about it all our lives. When we drove up we had caught a glimpse of it through the opening between the *verksted* and *lager*, now we wanted to see it up close. We continued past the parked car, past the *verksted*, and there it was, wider and more impressive than I had imagined. Flocks of seagulls wheeled and dove into the water looking for fish and making a huge racket. On the far side of the river, as far upstream or downstream as we could see was a mountainous forest with no sign of human impact. Erik and I looked excitedly at each other. Fishing, swimming, boating, exploring: The possibilities were endless and I instantly knew the river was the key to a fairytale summer.

By now Nøve had caught up with us. She pointed just a few hundred meters upstream to a small stream that joined the Eidselva. "In Norwegian, it's called an *Aa*," she said. "And because of the *Aa*, the land around this inlet is called *Aaland*, pronounced "Oh-land."

"Our name!" cried Erik.

"Yes, as an adult, your grandfather took the name of the land he was born on, *Aaland*," Nøve replied, "And this was how we got our family name."

As our aunt turned to walk back to the house, we dipped our hands into the clear water. It was freezing cold! *Bestemor* had also come out of the house looking for us. We heard her anxiously calling our names. In her limited English she told us to be careful. The river was deep and ran swiftly and she worried for our safety. I stepped back and took a breath. Even though I was born in San Francisco, there was no question I was an Aaland. This was my home and this was the river in my backyard.

H.K. Aaland, my paternal grandfather, is shown on the far right posing with four workers from the verksted, or furniture factory. Circa 1940.

A color poster advertising my grandfather's furniture business.

We were never bored at *Aaland*. There was always something to do, somewhere to explore. During the frequent summer downpours, when the rain fell so thick we couldn't see across the river and even the birds looked for cover, we joined our grandfather in the *verksted* and watched him work. My grandfather always wore a tie, even when he ran the powerful saw driven by a central motor and old-fashioned ceiling belts. Along with the tie was the pipe, not always lit but almost always hanging from his mouth. He was an old-world craftsman, a perfectionist, and it was mesmerizing to watch him work. Every cut, every swing of the hammer, seemed effortless and natural.

One time I offered to help. "*Nei, nei, nei,*" he said impatiently as he watched me struggle with a handsaw. I was holding it all wrong, and as I pushed and pulled I pressed down on the saw with all my might, trying to make the cut quickly as possible to impress *Bestefar*. I didn't understand what he was saying, but by his critical look I was sure he couldn't understand why his son, my father, hadn't taught me the basics of carpentry. Finally he took the saw and showed me how to allow gravity to do most of the work.

On rainy days we explored the adjacent *lager*, the two-story building that stored and displayed the finished furniture like a small-scale Ikea. One day, outside a small room in the back of the *lager*, we discovered a plaque with our father's name on it. It read, *Kr. Aaland Radio*. The letters were formed by small holes drilled into a sheet of shiny metal. There was nothing inside the room except for scraps of paper and a desk. We were curious about what went on in the room but we had to wait for one of Nøve's visits from Oslo to find out.

"Your father was in the radio repair business," Nøve explained when we finally got a chance to ask her. "He was self employed and ran the business until he left Norway after the war."

I always knew my father was keen on radios—he had them scattered all over the house in Livermore—but it wasn't until I was much older that I got the whole story about Dad and his radio repair business.

When my father was a boy, radios were new and novel. The first radio station in Norway broadcast in 1924, auspiciously the same year he was born. It soon became apparent Dad had an affinity for anything electronic, and that included radios. He was as natural with electrons and protons as our grandfather was with pine and birch.

On April 9th, 1940, when my father was 15 years old, the Nazis invaded Norway. My grandfather refused to collaborate, so his furniture business was appropriated and his workers sent home. German soldiers used my grandfather's tools and supplies to craft the bunks and furniture they needed for their barracks. My father didn't talk much about the war when we were growing up, but I knew it had been a tough time.

During the war it was illegal to own a radio. The penalty was death. Right under the soldiers' noses, behind a false wall, my father repaired radios for locals desperate to get news from the outside world. If Dad had been discovered, or if a single vacuum tube had been found in his pocket or stuffed into his hollow bike frame, he would have been shot on the spot, and then later, his family killed as well. He lived in constant fear, like many Norwegians did at the time.

After my father's death I asked Nøve about this time in his life. She admitted, "Your father had good reason to be scared. I don't think he ever quite got over it."

From left to right: Bestefar, Erik, Me,
and Tante Ingeborg in 1962.
Erik on our miniature KonTiki raft (insert).

In the spring of 1945, Germany surrendered unconditionally to the Allies and the war was over. The Nazis left Ulefoss and the country. Norway, poor to begin with, ended the war even poorer. My grandfather's business, which had been thriving before the war, was in a shambles. There was little work for young people, including my father. He continued his radio repair business, now openly, but in 1949 he jumped at the chance to go to sea as a ship's electrician and handyman. On the spur of the moment he decided to leave tiny Ulefoss and see the world. He left his small but growing radio business in the hands of his father, who promptly sold the remaining tubes, capacitors, resistors, and other parts, keeping only the metal plaque Erik and I found over a dozen years later.

As the days became shorter and the apples ripened, the last of the flowers in *Bestemor's* garden wilted. Before our dream summer ended in September and we flew back to Livermore, we were guests of honor at Nøve and her fiancé Sigbjørn's wedding. It took place at the Romnes Kirke, a 12th-century stone chapel on the outskirts of Ulefoss. Nøve wore her traditional *bunad*. My grandparents beamed with pride throughout the ceremony. On behalf of our father, who was in California, Erik and I happily welcomed Uncle Siggy, as we fondly called him, into the family.

On October 22, shortly after we returned home, President Kennedy went on national television and revealed the Soviet build-up of nuclear weapons on Cuba. He warned of a possible full-out nuclear confrontation. Our bomb shelter was nearly finished and my father rushed to make it ready, filling it with canned goods, medical supplies, and a Geiger counter. For a while we all slept in the shelter, but as the Cuban Missile Crisis ebbed, the others moved back upstairs. I stayed, making it my bedroom until I left for college. It was quiet, dark and private; in other words, it was a perfect bedroom for a teenager wanting privacy from his family.

A lot has happened between that summer in 1962 and today. My grandmother, Anna Kristina, died unexpectedly in 1974 from a stroke at the age of 72. H.K. Aaland, my grandfather, passed of natural causes in 1981 at the age of 85. I saw him at the Ulefoss old-folks home a week before he died. By that time I was conversant enough in Norwegian to talk with him and understand what he had to say. When he died peacefully a week later, both my dad and Nøve were there. Both of them had a chance to say goodbye.

With *Bestefar's* death, the Aaland property passed on to my father and Nøve. My aunt wisely understood that sharing the property with her unconventional older brother would be a recipe for disaster, so she sold him her half. It was perfect timing for my father. He had just retired from the Lab and was in a position to travel between Livermore and Ulefoss, splitting his time between both places. Sadly that all ended when my brother took his life.

Dad always loved Norway, but I am convinced he was also haunted by his childhood. He saw his life of relative comfort and safety snatched away by the Nazis, who replaced it with a life ruled by fear. Fear infected him like a disease that was with him wherever he went. Nowadays Dad would probably be diagnosed with Post-Traumatic Stress Disorder (PTSD) and instead of building a bomb shelter he likely would have spent time on a therapist's couch. I have no doubt Dad passed the fear on to me. Like father, like son. I didn't build a bombshelter, but I did grow up in one, which in turn led me to Kazz and his peace project. But that is another story. What is important now is to figure out what compelled Hans to do what he did. Did *Kr. Aaland Radio* have anything to do with it?

In the middle of January, a month after
my father's death, I travel alone to Norway with half my
father's ashes. As long as the ashes are in a sealed container
in my hand luggage and accompanied by a death certificate,
I am within the airline's rules. Technically I should declare
the cremated remains when I arrive in Norway, but I've been
advised that this could complicate matters with the custom
authorities. After a brief stopover in Amsterdam, I land at
the Oslo Gardermoen airport and proceed to the Nothing
to Declare line and cross my fingers.

"Dad, you are home," I mutter to myself as I exit the airport
without being stopped. Then I remember only half of him is
here. He now has one foot in his homeland and one in his
adopted country, almost literally at the same time. Death has
given him something he couldn't fully have in life.

Nøve meets me with open arms at the Lunde train station,
a 10-minute drive from Ulefoss. She has aged noticeably
since I saw her four months ago. Her beautiful blond hair is
gone, felled by chemotherapy, and she is wearing a wig. My
fondness for her, which started when I was very young, has
only grown.

"I am doing ok," she says matter-of-factly, and leaves it at
that. When Sigbjørn and I are alone, he tells me it is ovarian
cancer and that it has spread. Her prognosis is not good.
"Your aunt is stubborn," he says, "and she'll do her best to
beat it." I believe him. Stubborn runs deep in our family.

Nøve and I have had several long-distance phone calls about
my father's death, and there isn't much left to say. Instead
we give each other knowing looks that communicate our

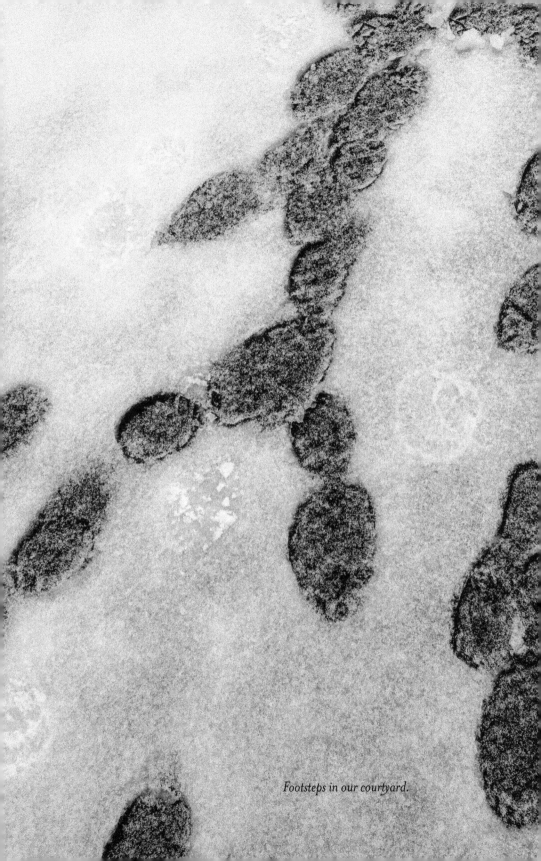

Footsteps in our courtyard.

common sadness. I am surprised she is not angry with Hans. Instead she wants to know how he is doing and whether or not he is being treated well. She is angry at the way the local press reported her brother's death.

"They printed his name and mentioned that Hans was mentally ill," she complains. "They didn't need to do that. It is not right."

When it comes to reporting crime and accidents, the Norwegian press is very circumspect and respectful of privacy, and rarely names names. A typical story might run, "A 30-year-old man from Skien was arrested Tuesday for robbing the Holla bank," and not provide any more detailed identification on the suspect even though the information is available to them.

My aunt's reaction makes me uneasy. Even though I have serious misgivings about the press coverage in the States, I would prefer to have the story out in the open rather than kept hidden and subject to misleading gossip.

Nøve drops me off in Ulefoss, and promises to pick me up early the next morning. I am left standing alone in the courtyard of the family home, surrounded by junked cars and rusty parts covered by a light layer of snow. I see my childhood fairytale shattered, and sigh. What a mess!

I carry my luggage into the *lager*, then walk across the frozen courtyard to the house, where my father's renters, Hans and Miriam, are waiting. When Dad inherited the property 23 years ago he needed extra income, so he divided the main house into two rental units and remodeled the *lager* so he had a place to stay. Hans and Miriam are worried about their future in the house. I assure them that I have no plans to sell the family property, and that they can stay. For now, I have decided nothing will change.

Back in the *lager* I have the choice of several bedrooms. My father, an incessant builder who believed in redundancy, added three sets of stairs, converted several of the storeroom spaces into bedrooms, and installed two kitchens. Several of the first-floor rooms are full of caustic-smelling, leaky hydraulic car parts. I avoid these and choose a room on the second floor at the back of the *lager* with an amazing view of the river and the mountains. It has a small kitchen and wood-burning stove. The kitchen sink is filled with dirty dishes, and there is a plate with a knife and fork on the table. Several improvised hearing aids hang from a nail. Dad's bed is covered with a thick down comforter, or *dyne*. It smells smoky, just like him. I snuggle up under it with a steady fire roaring beside me. I wake twice to pee and to add wood to the fire, but otherwise I sleep soundly, dreamless.

Nøve shows up early the next day. With the death certificate in hand, and with Nøve's help, I'm amazed by how easy it is to transfer the property into my name. I am my father's eldest son, yes, but I am an American, born in San Francisco and technically a foreigner. I thought this process would be complicated, but it doesn't seem to be.

After just two days I am finished. The property is officially mine; I am the fourth-generation Mikkelsen/Aaland to hold the deed. Nøve drops me off at the house again and asks if I want to join her and Sigbjørn for dinner. I politely decline; I need some time alone. We agree on dinner the next night, before I leave for Oslo and home to San Francisco.

Hans the renter is on the porch smoking a hand-rolled cigarette. After a brief chat, he goes back inside. He wants to reassure me that he will watch over the property when I am back in the States, just like he did for my father. I am grateful, as I will need all the help I can get.

At the far end of our property next to the river is a covered swing, a heavy metal structure my father built from a Citroën chassis. It sits at the exact spot Erik and I stood when we were kids and first felt the magic pull of the river. I walk to the swing through the snow-covered courtyard. It is surrounded by cars, disembodied windshields and mufflers, but sitting in it I have an unobstructed view of the river.

I swing back and forth and close my eyes. The last few days have gone well, but I am spent. I feel like all the weight in the world has shifted from my father onto my shoulders. My father's death has removed a barrier that separates me from my own death. I breathe and try to relax. It helps to look beyond the discarded car parts to the silent river flowing in front of me. I turn my focus on my steamy breath.

Inhale, exhale. Inhale, exhale. Slow and steady.

Then a refrain from the Steve Miller Band song *I Want To Make The World Turn Around* pops into my mind. I have liked this song since it was released in the 1980s.

> *I don't want to live in a world of darkness,*
>
> *I want to live in a world of light,*
>
> *I don't want to live in a world that's heartless,*
>
> *I want to live in a world of sight,*
>
> *Well you know, I want to make the world turn around,*

I repeat the lines over and over, and as I do I imagine a pale, shimmering light surrounding me, the river, and this town. The image comforts me, and for a few precious moments I feel at peace with the world. My attention shifts from the river back to the chaos around me. Suddenly, instead of protecting me, the shimmering light marks me as a target for bad things, and a dark chasm filled with ghostly shapes opens in front of me. The change from comfort to fear is swift, and

I feel vulnerable and scared. Yet while I struggle with these troubling thoughts, the river continues to flow, quiet and steady in front of me. All I have to do is turn my attention back to it to find comfort again.

1 4

Shortly after I return from Norway, in February, Erik calls and says he just drove Mom to the Kaiser hospital in Walnut Creek. He thinks it's a stroke, but the next day the doctor tells us her dizzy spells are due to a failing heart valve. He says there are two choices: open-heart surgery to repair the valve, or nothing, in which case he gives her six months to a year.

"I would not recommend surgery if it were my own mother," the doctor replies to our question.

There are some promising, less-invasive techniques for repairing heart valves, but they are still experimental, and only available in Europe. Mom agrees with the doctor and is adamantly against the surgery. She doesn't want to risk living her remaining time in a hospital bed or a wheelchair in a rest home. She wants to take her chances and do nothing. This turns out to be a great choice, as she will go on to live another seven years, all independently.

She is released from Kaiser the next day. When I pick her up she is happy to take Rebecca and me up on our offer to stay with us in San Francisco for a few days. She has been staying with a neighbor in Livermore, but the stress of dealing with the still red-tagged house is getting to her. She is considering selling the house instead of making all the repairs required by the building inspectors. She visits Hans every week. He is still at the Santa Rita Jail, just outside Livermore. He has his own cell and is still on suicide watch.

"He is awfully thin," she says once we get home and she settles into her preferred spot at the kitchen table by the window. "He is not eating. He spends all his time reading the Bible."

Then she says something that sends a shiver down my spine.

"Your father was getting old and he was slowing down. His shoulder and knees were bothering him a lot. Hans didn't like him in pain. It might have been..."

"For the best?" I finish incredulously. "Are you kidding?" my voice rising. "Don't go there. He had years left."

Then I'm standing, yelling, "Don't ever say that again!"

She looks downcast and meek. I sit down, and my voice gets softer.

"Please Mom, don't ever say that again. Even if it is coming from Hans."

"I am sorry. It's not what I believe."

"Hans had no right to do what he did. None. I don't care how skinny he is. I don't care if Dad was on his deathbed. He had no right."

"I know, I know," she says.

And then she adds, "But please, promise me you will go and see him."

"Mom!" And then I look at her and see tears in her eyes. I feel guilty for making her feel bad. Reluctantly, I promise to see Hans, even though the thought of facing my brother brings back all the pain and makes me feel ill.

The truck my father built for carrying heavy loads to
Pi Pi Valley in the California Sierra. The engine hood
is a refrigerator door. Circa 1969.

Visiting hours are limited at the Santa Rita Jail, so the parking lot is nearly full when I arrive. Rebecca offered to come but I feel I need to do this alone. It is a weekday in March, four months after my father's murder. I join a long line of women and children stretching from the main entrance out to the street. I am the only man there. As the line slowly moves I nervously finger the amulet hanging from a string around my neck. Kazz gave it to me many years ago to ward off evil spirits and to bring luck. It consists of one vertical line with a bar running to the left and farther down another bar running right. If the two sidepieces were slid to meet one another, it would form the Christian cross.

"The sidepieces are in the process of becoming," explained Kazz. "For Shintoists, process is very important. When you observe something in motion you see its true nature."

I am not normally superstitious and I haven't worn the amulet in years. But these are not normal times. I have never visited someone I know in prison before. I feel so embarrassed, like the whole world is watching me. How does my mother do this week after week? And at her age? If she can manage it, then so can I. I have put it off long enough, and a promise is a promise.

Finally, after registering with the prison guard and storing my cell phone, keys, camera, and wallet in a locker, I face Hans through a thick Plexiglas window. Except for a brief glimpse of him in shackles and an orange jumpsuit at his court arraignment a few weeks after he killed Dad, this is the first time I've seen him since Thanksgiving. He is thin and pale, just like my mom said. The thick, yellowed window distorts his face.

Even in his current condition, anyone can see we are brothers. We both have blond hair, blue eyes, and are tall and slender. We are woven from the same DNA and upbringing, but inside the weaves came out different. We both had issues with our father, but I never even fantasized about killing him. Hans actually suffocated him.

At first we are without words, and just look at each other. His eyes are cloudy and masked and I can't see beyond his pupils. What is lurking back there? What is he hiding? For a moment I imagine bad spirits in control, and I am thankful to have the amulet around my neck.

He breaks the silence first. "Thank you for coming." For an instant he becomes my baby brother again.

I nod, lean forward, and ask how he is doing.

"I'm fine," he says. But he turns his head this way and that and appears a bit disoriented. Are they giving him antipsychotic drugs?

"Are you getting any exercise, any fresh air?" I ask, concerned.

"I am not looking for sympathy," he says, slurring slightly. "I'm fine, really I am."

"They had you on suicide watch for awhile," I say.

"That wasn't necessary," he replies.

I want to ask him why he killed our father, but before I can he says, "You know I love Dad. I did what I had to do. God told me to do it."

He has been consistent with his reasoning, always saying he simply did what God asked him to do. He has chosen a heavenly father over his flesh and blood one. I am stunned at how nonchalant he is. "I had a dream about Dad last night. He said he forgave me. He understands."

How do I respond? This is a new nightmare. On the one hand, he looks so pitiful and harmless sitting behind the Plexiglas. On the other hand, I am scared of him. Is he contagious? Can bad spirits fly through the glass? I want to run from the jail and never see him again. He has both destroyed and shamed our family but shows no remorse. He can stay locked up for ever, as far as I am concerned.

I leave the prison shaken. It is clear he cannot give me a satisfactory answer as to why he did what he did. For now I have to look elsewhere for answers. I also have to find a way to inoculate myself from his disease and protect my girls.

1 6

Hans is officially diagnosed as paranoid schizophrenic during the summer of 2005 and declared unfit to stand trial. He is transferred from Santa Rita Jail to the Napa State Hospital. I learn about his status from my mom on a phone call while I am in Ulefoss with Rebecca and the girls. She tells me her health is ok as long as she doesn't push herself. With the help of a kind family friend, who happens to be a realtor, she has managed to sell her red-tagged home "as is" to a speculator. I am relieved on all counts. No matter how I feel about my brother, prison is a horrible place for him and the psychiatric hospital in Napa is a big improvement. With money in the bank, my mother can now afford to move into an apartment and put some distance between herself and the scene of the crime.

The clean up in Norway proceeds slowly, largely because we only have two months before the girls need to be back to school in San Francisco. We clear buckets with random shards of glass and remove leaking car parts from the garden.

Rebecca plants grass where the derelict cars used to be, and flowers. With the help of several friends we fill two dumpsters and make countless trips to the landfill. When we fly back to San Francisco in August I'm exhausted, but there is still plenty more to do in the future.

We settle back into the familiar routine in San Francisco. School, field trips, ballet, piano lessons, and martial arts classes. Rebecca is enrolled in an intensive Iyengar yoga teaching program, and regularly contributes travel articles to local magazines. I take on photo assignments, lead workshops, and write photography how-to books and articles.

The river of my life flows steadily in a new direction, but I don't know where it is going. I miss the phone calls and surprise visits I used to get from my father as he traveled back and forth between Livermore and Norway. Discussions with my mom are nearly always about Hans and his current status. My brother Erik, on the other hand, refuses to see him and doesn't want to talk about Dad's death. The temperature in Ulefoss drops below 0°C and I call the other Hans in Norway. He assures me the pipes are fine, but I still worry.

The summers of 2006 and 2007 are repeats of 2005. Our renters Hans and Miriam still occupy the main house. We sleep in the *lager*, avoiding the first floor, where the smell of brake fluid lingers. We spend a lot of time cleaning and tidying up and the place is looking better. It is not all work. We are in a beautiful place and a simple walk through the woods is a rejuvenating experience. Despite everything, we have it pretty damn good.

Back in San Francisco in the late fall of 2007, I receive a long-distance call from Miriam in Ulefoss. She tells me that a subsidized apartment in town has just became available, and that she is calling to give notice. She will move out in January. Hans will remain upstairs, but Miriam's leaving means I have to find a replacement tenant.

When I tell Rebecca, she replies, "We don't need to find someone to replace Miriam. Let's take it ourselves."

Ever since Miranda and Ana were born we've talked about living overseas for a year to give our girls an international experience. Staying in the *lager* was never an option. It is fine for summer visits, but it's not insulated for the long, cold Norwegian winter.

"Now is the perfect time," Rebecca adds.

She is right. Ana is seven and Miranda eleven; they can easily do a year of school in Norway without interfering with their education. When they are older and more attached to their friends, it will be much more difficult to try and pry them away.

"Yeah, that makes sense. We can rent our apartment in San Francisco," I say, recalling how easy it has been to get renters for each of the last three summers. We don't have a mortgage in Norway, and as long as we live frugally, we can make the move financially feasible. I can easily work from anywhere with an Internet connection. Rebecca is a certified Iyengar yoga instructor now and can add to our income by teaching. It will give her one more year with the girls before she needs to return to work full time.

Leaky paint can (left) and removal of one of my father's Citroëns.

Once we make the decision to go everything quickly arranges itself. Hans, our upstairs renter in Norway, agrees to keep an eye on the empty downstairs apartment until we arrive in the summer of 2008. Through Craigslist we find the perfect family to sublet our home: a Swiss family with two young boys. The husband is a banker on a one-year assignment to San Francisco and he can walk to his job in the financial district from our apartment.

Our daughters' teachers are enthusiastic about the year abroad and assure us places will be available for them when we return. Both my and Rebecca's mother are supportive. They know how quickly a year passes and each of them talks about making a trip to visit us while we are abroad. My mom's health is waning but she is still active, visiting my brother at Napa State Hospital and volunteering for symphony charity events. Erik has moved in with her and will keep an eye on her while we are gone.

Although practical matters are falling into place, my spiritual life still needs help.

1 7

By now it is early 2008. I haven't heard from Kazz in a year. It's not like him to be silent for so long, and I am worried. I also crave his advice. I have been busy the past few years cleaning the family property on the river in Norway, but I am at loss about what to do with the family river, the spiritual one Kazz said I needed to clean.

Just when I decide to make a phone call to Japan, I get an email from him. He explains he has been ill, and in and out of the hospital. At first he didn't know what was causing his heavy cough, fatigue, dizziness, and memory loss. He was finally diagnosed with a serious sinus infection. After an extensive operation he was released from the hospital, and he has been healing ever since.

"I am making my body stronger," he writes. " Hopefully soon I will be well enough to travel to Mt. Kailash."

The reference to Mt. Kailash is not out of the blue. For as long as I have known Kazz, he has talked about making a pilgrimage to Mt. Kailash, a holy mountain in the remote western corner of Tibet, near the borders of India and Nepal. The mountain is sacred to one out of every five people on the planet, yet few in the West have even heard of it; I never had until Kazz told me about it. Buddhist, Hindu, Jan, and Bon pilgrims believe that walking around Mt. Kailash on foot is a holy ritual that brings good fortune and washes away all sins. Kazz, as a Shintoist, also shares this belief. He has already made the pilgrimage once before, when he was in his early 30s, but feels he must return once more before he dies.

Even though the pilgrimage sounds strenuous and challenging, I am envious of his plans for the mountain. He doesn't fully explain why he wants to go, nor ask if I want to come, but I am sure he would welcome me as a companion. For obvious reasons, a ritual that brings good fortune and washes away all sins sounds very attractive to me. Unfortunately, I have so much on my plate that it can only be a fantasy. Kazz, on the other hand, has four grown daughters, is separated from his wife, and lives alone. There is little holding him back from making the journey, except his health.

I am relieved to finally hear from my dear friend. Now that we're back in communication, I press him for ways to ritualistically clean the family river.

"My father left a mess," I say. "It is a lot of work, but I know what to do to clean it up. From a spiritual point of view, however, I have no idea how to make things right."

Kazz quickly writes back and suggests I call a family meeting.

"You should ask your ancestors for help, " he explains. "It doesn't matter that they are all dead, their spirits are very much alive. Even though they have human failings, they can help. Maybe they can give you an idea of why your brother did what he did and what you should do next."

When I first visited Kazz in Japan, I remember him telling me about these ritualized family meetings. Even though I like the idea of honoring the dead in our everyday lives, it is a stretch for me to accept an invisible world of spirits where the dead are literally alive, or at least aware. Now that I am older I appreciate that there is so much I don't know. When I ask myself whether I believe in the spirit world I have to answer, why not?

In response to my questions about the proper way to conduct an ancestor meeting, Kazz sends me simplified instructions a Westerner like me can follow. He says I can do the ceremony in my own home, but first I must thoroughly clean the room I use.

"You must be prepared when you contact the spirit world," explains Kazz. "You don't want deceitful spirits to interfere and cause confusion or trouble."

He explains that I need to select and gather objects favored by my ancestors. The objects should represent something they like. I choose chocolate for my father. For my father's father I choose a pipe, and for my father's mother I choose flowers. For my mother's mother, Ester Goodson, I choose bath salts, and for my mother's father, George Arthur Goodson, whom I never met, I pick a golf ball; my mom has told me he loved to play golf and was quite good at it.

One day in late April, when Rebecca and the girls head off

to visit her mom and stepfather in Berkeley, I prepare for the family meeting. I vacuum and straighten the living room and then place the chocolate, pipe, flowers, golf ball, and bath salts on a table in the middle of the room. My father built the table many years ago out of a slab of aluminum and other parts he picked up at a Lab junk sale. In the middle of the pile of favored objects I balance a 12-inch leafy branch from our backyard that Kazz told me to stand upright, like a Christmas tree.

I sit quietly for a few moments and then, as Kazz suggested, I identify myself out loud as someone who worked with him and his *sensei*, Takizawa Hakuryu. Then I call out to my ancestors by name, one by one.

I am surprised by what happens next. I had expected my mind to be filled with warm, supportive images of my relatives jumping in and offering advice and help. Isn't that what relatives are supposed to do? Instead I find my head full of needy people, all wanting attention. Strangely, I have no sense of my father. For some reason I can't conjure up a clear image of him. Maybe it's still too soon.

Faced with so much neediness, I become defensive, and not at all respectful. I begin by questioning my Norwegian grandfather. "You wanted me to speak better Norwegian, but did you try to learn English?" With my American grandfather I am even harsher, asking him why he died when my mother was so young. Was he really an alcoholic, as my mother used to say? To my mother's mother I say bluntly that I never liked when she signed her letters to me "Princess." I ask my father's mother why she was always hovering over us as kids, not letting us climb trees and always overly protective?

The irony is not lost on me that I am wide-awake and hearing and talking to voices that seem very real. It feels like a thin line separates me from sanity and madness, or even my brother Hans' delusions.

Bestemor and Bestefar on their wedding day, 1923.

After a few minutes I recognize that my accusatory tone isn't getting us anywhere, and I apologize for my disrespect. It suddenly occurs to me my ancestors are in as much shock about what happened between my father and my brother as I am. I hear only silence when I ask them what they think I should do.

At the beginning of our meeting, I wanted so much to be taken care of. But now I realize my ancestors need to be taken care of too. Clearly, we need to do this together. At the end of our meeting I bow my head in thanks, and as Kazz instructed, drive the leafy branch to the beach, where I toss it into the Pacific Ocean.

Afterwards I write and tell Kazz I didn't get what I hoped for from the meeting.

"They wanted things from me and didn't seem to have anything to offer in return," I explain.

"Maybe you surprised them," he writes back. "They don't understand what you are doing. You have to explain things to them, bring them slowly on board. Then try asking for advice another time."

We will leave for Norway in a couple of months. Rebecca has ordered a half-crate to ship some of the things we will need for our year overseas. Along with winter clothes, and my girls' toys, I add a stack of books and photography magazines that I've been meaning to read for months. I am both excited and anxious. Stretching in front of me are two rivers to explore. One is very real, very beautiful, and literally flows in my backyard. The family river flows in my veins, now stained with patricide. Both rivers, I hope, will help explain to me the mystery of why my brother did what he did.

Maybe then I will know what to do next.

Flåvatn, upriver from our home in Norway.

PART 2

The river is everywhere.

— *Herman Hesse, Siddhartha*

20 JUNE 2008

My family and I have just spent 20 hours flying over North America, Iceland, and the North Atlantic, followed by a two-and-a-half-hour train ride south from Oslo to Lunde in a sleek, modern train car. Uncle Sigbjørn meets us at the station and drives us to Aaland in Ulefoss, our home on the river. We have so much luggage that my uncle has to make two trips from the station with his Volvo. It is really hot for Norway, about 28° C (82°F). It is nearly the summer solstice, the longest day of the year, and the sky doesn't get dark.

After three summers of traveling back and forth between San Francisco and Norway, Ana and Miranda are, at seven and eleven years old, seasoned travelers. Moments after we unload, they slip into swimming suits and jump into the icy cold river, unfazed by the long journey.

Rebecca immediately gets to work pulling up dandelions and other weeds from the gravel courtyard and garden, a satisfied look on her face. I'm happy to be here too, but when I look around I just see all the hard work ahead. The junked Citroëns and spare parts that were distributed throughout the property are mostly gone, but now we need to focus on the smaller-scale cleaning tasks and the long overdue maintenance like painting and a new roof. I also see myself continuing to do what I have been doing, writing, taking photographs, and trying to

Aaland

Hans, our father, and a Citroën,
circa 1968.

solve a murder mystery. It's not a who-done-it mystery—we all know my brother killed Dad—but a why mystery. Why did he do it? Lots of people are mentally ill and they don't kill their parents. I feel there is more to this.

Here at the birthplace of my father, with a treasure chest of family history and lore surrounding me, I hope to get to know my ancestors better and find more clues to my brother's behavior. Aging photographs, 16mm film, letters, and living relatives are all within easy reach. I have a year on the river to burrow through it all. I have no idea what I will find.

To walk along the narrow, low-ceilinged, hallways of the *lager* is to walk through time. My father hung family pictures everywhere on the walls of what used to be my grandfather's furniture store. Many of the pictures are of Dad as a young man—he had no qualms about viewing himself— but there are plenty of photographs of my grandparents, aunts, uncles, and cousins, as well as of my mom, and my brothers and I when we were young.

I stop and stare at a color photograph of Hans at probably 10 or 11 years old, with my father. Dad is standing and Hans is kneeling; they are in front of a Citroën, the French cars my father declared a technological masterpiece. With its hydropneumatic suspension and air tunnel design, the Citroën is a strange-looking car, way ahead of its time. "It doesn't glide on the road," Dad liked to brag, "It flies on air." In the picture, the Citroën is parked in our front yard in Livermore, and I get a chill when I look at it and realize that 50 years later my father's half-naked body would end up sprawled nearby.

Back then Hans was a normal kid. I was quite fond of him, even though my first memory of him is colored by his non-stop crying. It started the day he came home from the hospital. He cried so much at night that our father shut him in a small closet. I was six years old, years before I moved into the bomb shelter, and none of the bedrooms were far apart. I lay in the top bunk unable to sleep because of his muffled yet maddening howls. I was sure my parents heard him from their bed, but they didn't do anything. Later, when I am older and ask Mom about it, she tells me she wanted to get up and do something but Dad told her to let him be.

"He felt Hans needed to learn to comfort himself," she says. "And we needed the sleep."

Hans' crying seemed to go on forever, but after a few months it stopped. In my young mind, Hans was a squeaky wheel that constantly needed and got attention from our mom. I don't think she loved him more than she loved Erik and me, but I couldn't help noticing she shared a compatibility with him. It didn't bother me too much. I was more in step with my father.

As he grew older, it became clear that Hans had many talents. He had a great singing voice and played the lead in several high-school musicals, including "South Pacific" and "Music Man". He was popular with girls, who clucked protectively around him, and he was a high-school track star. I felt happy for Hans and proud to be his older brother.

Hans was much like the ultimately successful third-born portrayed in so many fairy tales, from *The Three Little Pigs* to Grimm brothers' *The Three Sons* to J.K. Rowling's *Beedle the Bard*. In Hans Christen Asbjornsen's Norwegian fairytale *The Ash Lad*, for example, the third son is smarter than his other brothers and outwits trolls, dodges charging unicorns, and uses a magic Viking ship to help him win the princess.

I can see the logic in these stories. In the olden days the eldest son always inherited the farm, while the second son got the money; the first two brothers were set. Nothing was left for the third son, so he had to make do with his wits. He was the one who thought outside of the box, he was the inventor and the visionary, while the older sons were at best conformist and conventional, and at worst scoundrels or thieves.

For Hans, everything changed in 1977 when he graduated from high school and went to live with a friend in Alaska. At nineteen, he was hired to work at a mental hospital in Anchorage—talk about irony—and started smoking a lot of strong marijuana. He quit his job the following spring and returned to Livermore to live with our parents. I have a memory of him that summer at the Alameda county fair, where I operated a photo studio, strolling through the midway strumming a guitar and singing Christian songs. I barely recognized my younger brother. Something had happened to him; he had met God.

Breakdown

The way he tells it, it was just after he returned from Alaska and he was walking on a beach near Carmel, California, smoking a joint. The sun set over the Pacific Ocean and suddenly he had the feeling that Jesus was talking directly to him, telling him to read the Bible. He calls it an awakening, but now, with hindsight, I see it as a psychotic episode and the start of his progression to full-blown schizophrenia.

At the time we simply thought he'd become a "Jesus freak," intent on saving souls. This was the '70s and mental illness was not as openly discussed as it is now. We thought Hans would grow out of his religious phase. Little did we know it wasn't a phase at all.

Minimization of Denial

As the years passed, Hans became even more fanatic, and increasingly called attention to himself. He handed out leaflets containing biblical verses throughout downtown San Francisco while riding a tall and elaborately decorated unicycle and wearing a flamboyant jester hat. He became increasingly aggressive about the Bible and in his conviction that God was speaking directly to him. Most conversations with Hans were about his delusions. He devised elaborate connections between numbers and letters, which he talked about non-stop. By then we obviously knew something was seriously wrong, but we didn't know what to do about it. We had no idea it would end so badly.

Sometime in the mid '90s I called the California Department of Social Services, only to learn we were dealing with a Catch 22. There was nothing we could do without Hans' permission unless we could prove he was a danger to himself, other people, or property. At the time we couldn't; he lived with our parents, held part-time jobs at various restaurants, participated in church activities, and was well-liked by many people, even if considered eccentric. Hans felt he didn't need help and that itself confirmed how serious his illness had become.

It is easy for me to feel guilty now, but at the time I could only do so much. I was busy starting a family, my brother Erik was overcoming personal difficulties and trying to get his life together. My parents were concerned but clueless about what to do. My mom bristled at the term schizophrenia, and Dad didn't really get mental illness at all. He thought Hans should just "get over it," whatever "it" was.

In March 2003 Hans was arrested for assaulting a police officer with a "deadly weapon" (a stick of wood he picked up from the ground) while riding his unicycle. He was also charged with resisting arrest and trespassing. He was institutionalized at a psychiatric facility, but was released after a few weeks and encouraged to seek therapy. He did attend a few sessions over the next six months, but by then he was deeply entrenched in his illness. He did not take any medication. A year later Hans received instructions from God to kill our father.

The only consolation I now find is that the wreck occurred within our own family, so that the collateral damage to the outside world was minimal. It could have been much worse. My father was the one who took the bullet, so to speak, but at least no one else had to.

Last night I dreamed that all the family pictures on the *lager* walls had been removed, including the photo of Hans and our father. Only blank walls remained. I felt alone and adrift, but also very light and free. Then, in my dream, Miranda and Ana appeared, staring at the empty walls. They turned from one wall to another, looking lost. Suddenly I was filled with profound sadness. I can't escape the past, I thought. The future won't let me.

20

At lunch I'm irritable and I snap at my daughters and wife when I find their dirty breakfast dishes in the sink. I eat my lunch alone outside, next to our neighbor Leif's fruit-laden cherry trees, swiping angrily at the wasps buzzing my pasta dish. The sun feels strong and good, and the earthy smell of our freshly cut lawn surrounds me. I try to talk myself into a better mood, but I'm like a dog chasing its tail. No matter what I do, I can't stop disturbing thoughts from entering my mind.

I am furious with my father for leaving behind such a mess, and furious with my brother Hans. I'm also furious at the fate that put me here to literally clean up after my father and somehow clean up after my brother, too.

My anger at both of them merges into a single stomach-wrenching emotion. From the feelings simmering wordlessly

The Ulefoss iron works.
Canal boat and locks (insert).

and unarticulated beneath the surface of my conscious mind, a seething thought emerges: Did my father get what he deserved? Did he provoke Hans in some unidentified way?

I finish my lunch and flee to the *verksted*, the barn-like structure that housed my grandfather's furniture workshop. All the heavy woodworking machinery is gone. I've swept, dusted, washed, recycled the leaky paint cans, and organized a small office space complete with a desk and photo printer. I look through the windows to the steadily flowing river. Was Dad responsible for his own death? I will only feel safe when I find the answer.

2 1

I'm in the basement of the family home. It's Saturday morning, and there is a chill in the air even though it is only August. I hear my two girls playing in the room above me. They are happy, and that makes me happy.

The basement is full of dirt, dust, and mold from years of neglect. I've already made several trips to the local dump with garbage. I am wearing a mask, but I can still smell the noxious dust that makes it past the filter into my lungs. First I sweep the concrete floor, then spray the concrete walls with diluted vinegar to kill the mold. I fill bucket after bucket with water from the river and wash the floor and walls using a biodegradable cleaner. I empty each bucket over the gravel in the back near the river, and start again. When I'm finished I sprinkle sea salt on the walls and on the floor, enacting an ancient Japanese purification ritual, another of Kazz's suggestions.

I'm doing all the purifying I can, and covering all my bases.

I need to know more about schizophrenia: What is it exactly? Why was my brother affected? Is it an inherited trait? Am I or my daughters at risk? Is there a cure? I spend countless hours on the web and with books researching this incredibly complex mental illness.

According to the National Institutes of Health, schizophrenia is a chronic, severe, and disabling brain disorder that has affected people throughout history. Symptoms include hearing voices other people don't hear, paranoia, delusions, disorganized thought, and depression. Because of the severity of its impact, it has been called the cancer of mental illness.

Contrary to what I originally believed, a schizophrenic isn't someone with a split personality, or who exhibits two or more distinct personalities. *Schizo*, from the German, refers to a split or breakdown in the thinking process, which results in a perceptual disconnect between what is real and what is imaginary; *-Phrenia* refers to the mind. A schizophrenic displays confused and/or delusional behavior and might laugh when something bad happens, or believe they are Elvis.

Paranoid schizophrenia—my brother's official diagnosis following his arrest—refers to a type of schizophrenia complete with delusions and non-existent voices, but with less-noticeable symptoms, such as loss of memory or concentration. My brother fit this definition by killing our father in the belief that his act would save the world, but still being quite capable of carrying on a perfectly normal conversation, and even recalling childhood events that I had forgotten.

(Although paranoid schizophrenia is defined in the 4th Edition of the Diagnostic and Statistical Manual of

Mental Disorders, the American Psychological Association dropped it from the 5th Edition in 2013. They eliminated schizophrenia subtypes because "they did not appear to help with providing better targeted treatment, or predicting treatment response.")

Schizophrenia directly and indirectly affects millions of people in all countries and cultures around the globe. In the U.S. it directly affects one percent of the population, but it occurs in ten percent of people who have a first-degree relative with the disorder, such as a parent, brother, or sister. People who have second-degree relatives (aunts, uncles, grandparents, or cousins) with the disease also develop schizophrenia more often than the general population. Schizophrenia can be somewhat controlled through pharmacology, and to a lesser degree talk therapy, but at this time there is no cure. Treatment is most effective when begun soon after the onset of symptoms.

I learn that men in late adolescence and early adulthood are particularly susceptible to schizophrenia; Hans first exhibited the symptoms in his late teens. Women are affected by schizophrenia in equal numbers as men, but they first exhibit symptoms at a later age. Schizophrenia rarely manifests itself after the age of 45, statistically putting me in the clear, but not my daughters.

Most people who suffer schizophrenia do so quietly, often taking medications that mute the symptoms. Only a few make headlines like my brother did by committing violent acts against others, although people with schizophrenia are nearly 20 times more likely to have committed murder than people in the general population. Schizophrenics are also more likely to do harm to themselves than others, and have a much higher rate of suicide than other groups.

It is commonly believed that genes, environment, and an imbalance in brain chemistry play a role in schizophrenia.

Even though recent studies have discovered several genetic markers associated with schizophrenia, it is still not clear why some people with the genetic markers get the disease while others don't. Drugs, especially marijuana, can trigger the onset of symptoms. Stress from within or without a family can also trigger the disease. Hans smoked marijuana as a teenager, and our father's seemingly constant hammering, grinding, and sawing was an obvious sign that there was tension within the Aaland family.

What about my daughters? Are they predisposed to schizophrenia?

Not necessarily, thank goodness. According to Andrew Solomon in his bestselling book, *Far from the Tree*, there are markers for vulnerability rather than guarantees of disease. He writes, "One member of a family with a defective gene can be schizophrenic, but another member with the same gene defect might be bipolar or severely depressed." Solomon continues, "Nobody knows what protects some gene carriers from the condition... Genetics most likely mix with environment to cause a shift in biochemistry, which then has a degenerative effect on brain structures."

Up to now I have been looking at schizophrenia from a Western medical point of view. Non-Western traditional cultures look at it differently; for the most part, they attribute mental illness to a lack of harmony between individuals and their environments, and to supernatural causes such as witchcraft and spirit possession. Journalist Ethan Watters writes in his thought-provoking book, *Crazy Like Us: The Globalization of the American Psyche*:

> We can become psychologically unhinged for many reasons, such as
> personal trauma, social upheaval, or a chemical imbalance in our
> brain. Whatever the cause, we invariably rely on cultural beliefs ands
> stories to understand what is happening. Those stories, whether they
> tell of spirit possession or serotonin depletion, shape the experience

of the illness in surprisingly dramatic and often counterintuitive ways. In the end, all mental illnesses, including such seemingly obvious categories such as depression, PTS, and even schizophrenia, are every bit as shaped and influenced by cultural beliefs and expectations as hysterical leg paralysis, or the vapors, or zar [Middle Eastern mental illness related to spirit possession], or any other mental illness ever experienced in the history of human madness.

In a chapter titled, "The Shifting Mask of Schizophrenia in Zanzibar", Watters reveals that on the East African island of Zanzibar schizophrenia is believed to be caused by spirit possession. I see similarities between the beliefs of my Japanese friend Kazz and what Watters is talking about.

These spirits that often inhabit living individuals aren't uniformly good or bad but can cause problems if they are not dealt with in appropriate ways. A spirit handed down from one's ancestors is generally thought to have a protective effect for the person who carries it. Such an entity will cause difficulties only if it is ignored or not properly appeased. These spirits can have an ethnicity, gender, and religious affiliation of their own. A spirit might be picked up accidently or through witchcraft. Sorcerers are said to raise and feed spirits, which they use to harm their enemies.

Spirits in Zanzibar are placated and their influences reduced by ritualized song and dance and with food or goods. Schizophrenia is therefore looked at as something transitory, not fixed or permanent. Rid a person of the bad spirits and they are free to live a normal life. According to Watters, "…spirit possession narratives kept the sick person within the social group. Importantly, the idea that spirits come and go allowed the person with schizophrenia a cleaner bill of health when the illness went into remission.

Watters cites an international study conducted by the World Health Organization over the course of 25 years that showed that "people with schizophrenia in developing countries appear to do better over time than those living in

industrialized nations." No one has yet found a convincing explanation for the cross-cultural differences and Watters bemoans the lack of follow-up to these startling conclusions.

Another interesting fact I learn from the Watters book is the way schizophrenia manifests itself in different cultures. In Judeo-Christian cultures, delusions and hallucinations are often religious and often include hearing the voice of God and delusions of grandeur, just as in my brother. In other cultures the delusions of grandeur are rarer and the delusions often involve a dead relative.

Now that I know more about schizophrenia, I see two distinct ways of looking at it. One places the cause of the disease largely on chemistry and a defective gene. It offers the hope that one day there will be a definitive test to detect the disease early on when it is most treatable. It also offers the hope of a preventative pill or procedure, or even—as farfetched as it seems—an outright cure. These technological advances will likely be too late to help my brother, but I appreciate what they mean to my daughters and their offspring and millions of others who possibly face a life sentence of mental illness.

The other way of looking at schizophrenia envisions a world where spirits and magical thinking abound, a world where ancestors are called upon to intervene in everyday life and rituals lead to miraculous remission. This way doesn't depend on the rational and quantifiable. It works directly from the human heart, and heals through compassion and intent and love.

I have no doubt that magical thinking has a place in the healing process for me and my family. I just don't know how.

At age 20, I have my own brush with mental illness and I see firsthand what happens when the brain suddenly goes awry. It's 1972, and the Vietnam conflict is raging. I am a sophomore at Chico State University, but unsure what to do with my life. I enjoy swimming on the college team and working for the student newspaper, but I have yet to settle on a major. I want to photograph and write but there is no single major that encompasses both and I don't see why I have to choose one over the other. I need a break from school but my draft number is 54 out of 365 and if I don't maintain a 2S student deferment, I will be easily drafted and it's off to the rice paddies of Southeast Asia. No one can convince me that war is worth dying or killing for.

I plead with sympathetic teachers and find a way to maintain the minimum class credit required to keep my full-time student status and still leave school well before the end of the semester. My father's cousin, Hans Jorgen Frank, whom my brother is named after, is the technical director of the Rosenberg shipyard in Stavanger, Norway. He has arranged a summer job there for me and one of my college roommates.

At a going away party in Chico, my roommate's girlfriend passes us a tin of Alice B. Toklas brownies.

"Have a nice trip," she says with a sly smile, knowing full well that the marijuana-laced treat will ensure that we will. And then she gives each of us a friendly goodbye peck on the cheek.

We fly from the West Coast to London on a $250 roundtrip charter. Halfway over the Atlantic, after ingesting the brownie and drinking a glass of white wine, I pass out in the bathroom. I wake up in my seat just before landing, dazed and surprised at how quickly the 11-hour trip went. I feel rested and ready for my adventure at the shipyard.

The shipyard is located on an island in the middle of Stavanger, a small but important town on Norway's west coast. Oil has just been discovered in the North Sea and the town is filling up with Texans who advise the Norwegians on how to extract it. There is not much else going on. After hitchhiking from London to Norway, we move into a small apartment on the island, a few hundred meters from the shipyard. A five-minute ferry ride connects us with the rest of town.

We show up for work and are issued white plastic hard hats, overalls, and protective goggles, then given a quick lesson in chipping welding slag, the vitreous byproduct of the arc welding process. I am quite familiar with welding and slag; I had my fill of it when I helped my father build the bomb shelter in the early 1960s. Chipping slag is mindless work, but we are paid good money and enjoy the people we are working with. There is not much else to do in Stavanger but work. When it's not raining, it's about to rain. The days are dreary and gray. For a Friday night thrill we take the ferry into town, buy a beer at the train station café, and watch passengers disembark from the Oslo evening train.

A few weeks after starting my job at the shipyard I am alone at the small apartment. It is late Sunday morning and my roommate is up and out. I am in bed reading *The Boston Strangler*, by Gerold Frank, a book I picked up at a youth hostel in Denmark. It is the true story of the brutal murders in the early '60s of 13 women in the Boston area. The suspect was Albert DeSalvo, an unassuming man who no one thought is capable of committing the crimes. The book establishes his guilt and paints him as banal but profoundly disturbed.

I am about 155 pages into the book when I suddenly feel nauseated. I jump out of bed and run to the bathroom to

Stavanger shipyard 1972.

splash cold water on my face. I look in the mirror and see that I am covered in sweat. I don't recognize myself. I'm confused and disoriented and feel like throwing up. I run outside to find my friend, but halfway through the door I realize I am only wearing my underwear. I come back inside and dress quickly before leaving again. My friend is nowhere in sight, so I jump on the ferry and wander around town for the rest of the day, feeling dazed and lost. I feel like I am watching myself in a movie.

When I go to work on Monday I seek out the shipyard doctor. I explain what happened and that I still do not feel like I am myself. He says I am probably homesick and tells me there is nothing he can do. My friend doesn't understand either; he just shakes his head when I try to explain what happened to me. A week later my father visits. When he and I are alone, I try to tell him what I am feeling. He seems to listen, but then responds with a story about how scared he was during the war. I've never heard him talk about the war this way. It is interesting, but why is he telling me this now? Does he think I am scared? When he leaves for the States a few days later I feel worse than ever.

As the weeks pass, I hold myself together, although with a thin thread. Finally, on a rainy weekend hike to the top of Preikestoen (Pulpit Rock) I have an epiphany that starts me on the road to recovery. I'm on a rock ledge overlooking Lysefjorden, the dramatic fjord that sparkles 1982 feet below, and suddenly the sun breaks through a cover of dark clouds; in my mind's eye I see a path to my future and happiness. I won't go as far to say I saw God, but I certainly had the feeling of something other, something that reached out and helped me help myself. I will return to college in the fall and take advantage of Chico State's special major program to propose a special major that reconciles my desire to become both a photographer and a writer. I will create a curriculum that includes writing and photography courses and call my bachelor program Photo-Journalism. I don't have to choose one over the other after all. My plan becomes a life preserver that I cling to as if my life depends on it, which in some ways it does.

After that inspiring moment on top of Preikestoen my anxiety eases. Upon my return to school in late August, I find supportive ears and my special major is quickly approved by a panel of administrators and faculty. I slowly return to "normal" and no longer feel detached. I vow to avoid pot and stay away from downer books like *The Boston Strangler*.

So exactly what happened to me? Is it related to what happened to Hans, albeit with a different outcome? To help answer that question, I turn to a licensed psychologist in San Francisco. After hearing my story—many years after the incident—he is convinced that I did not have a psychotic episode like my brother. He tells me I wouldn't be sitting here calmly asking the question if I did. He says what I experienced was probably more akin to a well-documented, and more common mental illness called dissociative disorder. Ten percent of the population suffers from it at some point or another. It's defined as a disruption in memory, awareness, identity, or perception, often resulting from some form of psychological trauma. At best it is a coping strategy, at worse it is debilitating and can lead to suicide. In my case, the marijuana-laced brownies may or may not have played a role, but reading the horrific story of the Boston Strangler probably set me off. Unlike schizophrenia, the psychologist tells me, the prognosis for dissociative disorder is good, and it often goes away on its own, as it did with me.

Whatever you call it, at the end of the day, I consider myself lucky. My brother Hans was not.

Possibly. But may also have been a high anxiety/panic attack state related to feeling thwarted in his college major plans, as once he figured that out he began to feel better.

112

I am reading Dr. Andrew Weil's book, *Healthy Aging*, which I shipped here along with other books and magazines from the States. I knew Andy back in the '70s and '80s. We shared a passion for sweat baths and he turned me on to solar eclipses. One passage from his book jumps out at me:

> *Rivers are like living organisms in that they have many different mechanisms to keep themselves healthy. You can dump sludge into a river and up to a point the river can detoxify itself and remain in good health... But if you keep dumping sludge, at some point you will exceed a critical level where natural purification mechanisms become overwhelmed and break down... [and] the river becomes sick. A river that appears hopelessly polluted is not beyond help. If you simply stop putting bad substances into it, eventually the levels of contaminants will drop to a point where the natural healing mechanisms revive... and the river cleans itself up.*

What I want to know is this: Can a family heal itself in the same way? And if so, what are the bad substances I need to stop putting into the family river? I am already doing all I can to rid Aaland of the toxic paint and petrochemicals left by my grandfather and my father. What about generations of stress and denial? What am I doing about that?

Rebecca and I go to the local police station to register. All foreigners who wish to stay in Norway more than 90 days must do this. The woman behind the window types my name into the computer. Then she looks up and says, "But you are a Norwegian citizen. It says here you left Stavanger in 1972." I stare at her, confused. Finally, I mumble some excuse for my ignorance and change the subject to my wife and daughters.

Because my father was Norwegian and I was born in the U.S. I am able to hold dual citizenship. But I only had until my 20th birthday to declare my intent to hold both. At that time, even though I'd fulfilled other obligations, such as living for an extended time in Norway, my understanding was that I needed to serve in both the Norwegian and American militaries for a total of nearly six years. This was the late '60s and early '70s—the height of the Vietnam War; enlisting in both militaries at that time seemed a huge price to pay so I didn't do anything. At least I don't remember doing anything.

Somehow the formalities took place in 1972 when I was working at the shipyard in Stavanger. I filled out a lot of forms…and I did leave Stavanger when I was twenty, so the dates fit. In any case, by living and working in Norway I declared my intent and thereby retained dual citizenship. I don't know how I fell under the radar or why the military requirements were never enforced.

My wife, an American, still has to register and pay the 3000 kroner ($500) fee, but all I have to do is inform the local tax office that I have moved back and I am set. Our two girls, as the children of a Norwegian, are considered Norwegians as well, and it's only a simple formality to get them passports.

Learning that I've always been a Norwegian citizen has changed the way I look at everything. I feel like someone who has just discovered he has a long-lost sibling. At moments I feel disoriented, even though most things haven't changed at all. A huge part of me is very much American, informed by a past as sure as apple pie. Then again, as a kid I wore hand-knit wool sweaters, ate oily sardine sandwiches on pumpernickel bread at lunch, and was thoroughly teased for my food, my clothes, and for being a towhead.

I have always been a product of both cultures but now I don't think of myself as just an American with Norwegian heritage. I'm American and Norwegian. I am a dual citizen, a hyphenated person of the world. I feel privileged and honored to carry both passports, and I see a world of new opportunities opening up for both my daughters and me. I am also nervous. Even though globalization and technology have shrunk the world and made it easier than ever to travel back and forth between two far-apart countries, I am now bound by the laws of two countries and torn between two loyalties.

My father left me yet another responsibility, but he also left me another gift. I hope I am strong enough to take advantage of it.

The fish nets are empty again: no trout, no perch. We haven't caught any fish all season, except an occasional *gjedde*, or pike. The *gjedde* is a large, hungry fish with an alligator-like jaw and sharp teeth. It eats everything in sight, even baby swans. Some people like the *gjedde* for its taste and sport, but most of the locals bemoan the loss of the other fish. Several attempts have been made to rid the river of this

Gjedde (pike).

fish, including cash incentives and even mass poisoning with rotenone. All have been unsuccessful.

There are many theories about the proliferation of the *gjedde*, but I don't think anyone knows for sure why they have spread upriver. The river is different now, that's for sure. Man-made dams carefully regulate the flow of the river all the way upriver to its origin. In the days of my grandparents the river flowed faster, largely to expedite the downward movement of logs destined for the Skien sawmill. The logs brought nutrients that fed a more diverse ecology, and in addition, fast water discouraged the *gjedde*, which prefer the still waters of lakes.

Another theory postulates that the demise of trout and other environmentally fragile fish came as a result of the buildup of household pollutants that flow directly into the river, along with the spring runoff of salt used to keep the icy roads passable. Some people believe *gjedde* were planted by German sport fishermen who relished the fight of the aggressive fish, as well as the taste. The war is long over but some people here still find fault with the Germans.

It is tempting for me to compare the invasion of *gjedde* with the evil that has invaded my metaphorical family river, but in reality it is just an opportunistic fish doing what it is programmed to do.

What I think is this: Even though my daughters make a face when they say *gjedde*, maybe it is time for us to look at the *gjedde* in another way. If Norwegians can turn gelatinous, lye-soaked *lutafisk* into a Christmas delicacy, think of what they could do with the *gjedde*. In the high-tech world they call this "featuring the flaw."

If I could only do this with what happened to my father.

Today is the annual Gvarv apple festival (Eplefest). Gvarv, 15 minutes from our home, is a small town famous for its apples and sweet cherries. My distant relative Halvor Holtskog and his wife Kari Nyhuus live here and own a large apple and plum orchard. They also run a popular art gallery next to their traditional farmhouse.

At the festival I run into Ståle, one of our neighbors from Lanna. He was once a teacher but a tumble from his roof left him with neurological damage and a lot of pain. He spends much of his time in physical therapy and taking contemplative walks around the river. He didn't know my father nor any of the circumstances around his death, but he does know our river very well so I'm eager to ask him questions. As we sit and talk, our children explore the festival on their own. Because of his injury Ståle talks very slowly and deliberately.

He tells me that they've been sending timber down from the mountains for over 500 years, long before the canal was built. In the old days they'd dam parts of the river and then in the spring release the dams, shooting the logs with great force over the shallow areas. In the 19th century the canal was built to control the waters and stop the periodic flooding of the riverside towns. It made moving the timber easier, but the work was still seasonal. Today that is no longer so; trucks run year-round, feeding an insatiable appetite for ever more timber. The heavy trucks destroy the public roads while the river sits quiet, used only for tourist boats in the summer.

"Worst of all," Ståle says, "we are forgetting. What happens when we want to send the logs down the river again? Will we remember how? What happens when we want the name for a particular part of the river and the name is no longer on our tongue? What happens when the river is no longer our friend and washes over us and floods us?" After talking with me for half an hour, Ståle says he is very tired and excuses himself. I get the impression he needs to go off and be alone with his thoughts.

I really enjoyed listening to Ståle and hearing the words come out of his mouth slowly and carefully like the slow-moving river in front of me. I see him a lot during the year—he is one of my wife's regular yoga students at the community center— but I never have another conversation with him specifically about the river or its timeless flow. Six months later, I run into him on the banks of the river. He seems to appear out of thin air, like a sound. We nod a greeting to each one another and go our separate ways.

His last words to me that day in Gvarv were, "Sometimes we need a good knock on the head to remind us what is important." And to that I say, Amen.

My father was careless with the old family photos. The ones he left framed on the wall are in good shape but in the *verksted* I've just found a pile of dusty old photos piled on top of each other in a cracked wooden bowl. Here is one of my father as a small child, sitting in a wooden rowboat squinting in the sun. The boat isn't in the river, it is floating in the middle of Lannavegen, the road in front of our house. I can see our neighbor Leif's *verksted* in the background. On the back of the photo, written in pencil is the note "1927 *storflom.*" I know this refers to the famous flood of late June 1927 when heavy snow runoff faraway in the Hardangervidda crashed over the locks and dams and flooded all of Ulefoss. My father was four years old at the time.

Tante Ingeborg and logs on the river, circa 1960. My grandfather and a trophy trout, circa 1958 (insert).

My father on Lanna road during the famous 1927 flood.

The photo reminds me that the calm and peaceful river I see every day in our backyard is only part of the picture. What if my neighbor Ståle is right and one day the river is unleashed from the dams and locks upstream and runs wild? I imagine thundering waterfalls splashing the tops of trees with icy mountain water and salmon running unimpeded upstream from the sea to spawn. Strangely, I am not upset by these thoughts. There are worse things to consider; and besides, we too have a boat.

Today Miranda is twelve years old. It's a school day and instead of having her take the bus, I drive her and Ana to school. In San Francisco my daughters are in the minority; most of their classmates are of Chinese heritage, so I never have trouble picking the girls out from a crowd at school. Their hair makes them stand out like a flare. Here it's the opposite: When they leave our car, I watch them blend in with their Norwegian classmates like pine needles in an evergreen forest.

When I was in seventh grade, just as my older daughter Miranda is now, I envied my classmate Mark Grayson, who had jet-black hair. My hair, like that of my daughters, was strikingly blond and I was embarrassed by how different I looked.

One day in the boys' bathroom, Mark came up to me and said he'd give anything to have my hair. I was shocked; he wanted my hair!

Now I have less and less hair, and it is grayer and grayer. I look at my young daughters and I don't want them to go through what I went through. I don't want them to compare themselves unfavorably to others. I want more than anything for them to appreciate and be proud of what they have and who they are. I worry it won't be easy for them. Not because of their hair, which everyone can see is beautiful, but because they carry the stigma of having an uncle who killed their grandfather. Will others judge them for this? Or more importantly, will they judge themselves?

3 0

It's the middle of November and I haven't sat by the river for some time. Recent rains have swollen the river to the rim of our concrete embankment. It's hard to believe we have been in Norway over six months, and are almost halfway through our stay here. Time, like the river in front of me, is flowing swift and sure.

The ground has been frozen, with a thin layer of ice covering the grass. But over the last few days we've had a thaw and today is absolutely beautiful, even though the sun is hardly above the horizon. A flock of Canada geese honks loudly as it heads south. We are losing over four minutes of sunlight each day. (In San Francisco, at the same time of year, we lose less than two minutes a day.) By December 21, the shortest day of the year, sunrise will be at 9:19 a.m. and sunset at 3:12 p.m. Waves lap loudly against the side of the wooden boat, which I must take out of the water soon, before winter really settles in.

A single fluffy feather floats past me down the river. One minute it is there, capturing my attention, the next it is gone, replaced by an empty rippling surface. I am left with the real question: Am I halfway in my search for the answer to my

My daughter, Miranda.

father's death? Or will my search go on forever, like the never-ending flow in front of me?

I sit quietly, carefully watching the surface to see what will float by next.

Even though it is 1° C (34° F) today, it feels much colder. My neighbor Tore, has a name for this: *hus kald*. This is when it is cold, but not cold enough to freeze the bone-penetrating dampness from the air.

As the days grow shorter and colder we build bigger fires in the stoves to keep warm. There are several stoves spread out among the three buildings that make up Aaland. A pleasant whiff of smoke is always in the air. We mostly use one stove in the house, where we sleep, and in the *verksted* I fire up a large oven my father built from an old electrical transformer box. On weekends we heat the sauna in the back of the *lager* with a woodburning stove.

I enjoy building fires and I have gotten very good at it. I start with a pile of small, dry twigs and yesterday's newspaper. When the kindling ignites I blow gently on the flame. At this point the flame is so fragile I have to be careful not to blow it out. I have learned that well-seasoned, split wood is the best fuel. Birch, which is very plentiful here, is suitable because it burns hot and clean. Pine, properly cured, is fine, too but it doesn't burn as hot or clean as birch. After a while the fire gains strength and takes on a life of its own. At this point just about anything I throw into the flames will be easily consumed.

On days when my spirit feels delicate and flickers like a fitful flame, I imagine I am tending a fire. I deliberately feed it positive thoughts and avoid negative ones. I stay vigilant until my life force roars back and then I feel I can face most anything.

3 2

My cousin Jon Anders stops by Aaland tonight for a chat and a sauna. He is on his way home to Oslo after visiting his parents in Lunde. He's the youngest of my dad's sister's three boys and about 16 years younger than me. He sang at my father's service in Livermore and has been extremely supportive of my attempts to find an answer to his uncle's death. Not only is he a talented Norwegian folksinger, he's also a doctor working at the Oslo University Hospital.

In the blazing hot sauna I tell him about Kazz's concept of family as river. I tell him that a Shintoist believes an event occurring upstream can carry downstream and affect later generations. I tell him how committed I am to cleaning the family river for the sake of my girls. I am not sure what he thinks of the concept.

After a long pause he responds. "Sounds like epigenetics. It's the latest in genetics and inheritance."

I look at him, puzzled.

"I just read a paper on it. Some people call it the study of ghost genes." He continues. "You know about genes, of course."

I do. My blue eyes, my receding blond hair, my big nose, my height, and even certain aspects of my personality, like my clumsiness, all come from a chemical database formed from

the union of my mother and father. But ghost genes? I never heard of them and now it is my turn to be intrigued.

"Up to now, "explains Jon Anders, "we thought of the gene as hard baked, and untouched by the way one lives. Genes are passed on from one generation to another but experience isn't. Increasingly there is support for the idea that a gene can hold a memory of something that occurs long after birth, and can pass that memory on to offspring who can then pass it on to their offspring."

Jon Anders pauses for a moment as I splash a ladle full of water on the red-hot sauna stones. A powerful blast of steam hits both of us. With his face buried in his chest, Jon Anders continues.

"What our ancestors ate, what they breathed, what they saw," he explains, "can have a direct effect on us. If our grandfather smoked, for example, even if we never met him we could still get lung cancer."

"How can that be?" I ask. "How can a memory be encoded into a gene?"

"We aren't quite sure how the mechanism works," answers Jon Anders, "but it does, and it isn't limited to environment or diet. Somehow the environment can turn our genes on or off and change the very make up of our cells. Even emotional trauma or stress can be passed on from one generation to another through these ghost genes."

At this point we both dart from the hot sauna and dive into the cool river water, just a few steps away. After a quick swim we settle into nearby chairs.

After a moment Jon Anders turns to me and asks, "It's not that different from what your friend is talking about, is it?"

We are quiet and turn our attention to the river in front of us, the river that holds the souls of both our ancestors. Whatever name you give it—family karma, or epigenetics, or ghost genes—I feel I am on the right track. By looking to the past for answers, I hope I can stop the claim of my brother's act on the future.

It was minus 5° C yesterday and today we wake to a balmy 2° C. I take our wooden rowboat out on the river for the first time this fall, and the last time before I pull it out of the river for the winter. The sky is filled with the morning sun—patches of blue interspersed with yellow clouds. The clouds move slowly from the southwest, which usually means that there is no rain or snow in the forecast, because the mountains to the west catch and block the moisture. When the wind comes from the south, however, it's often followed by rain, which slams into Norway after screaming across the flatlands of Denmark and the sea.

I row with purpose to the other side of the river to take photographs. I am only a few hundred meters from the shore and our house but I feel so far away from the rest of the world I could be on the moon. I let the boat drift with the current. I marvel at the sky, the birds, and the soft, warm wind. I drift until I am near the road. The sight and sound of so many people heading to work pulls me from my reverie. I remember all the things I have to do, all the errands I have to run, and row quickly the rest of the way back.

Last night I went with my aunt Nøve to Lunde and met Alf Haugland, renowned author and poet and a former classmate of my father. Haugland was born a year after my father, in 1924, and was a friend of his until the end. As we sit in the living room of the modest home, Haugland, with his chiseled face and thick white hair, tells me he was as shocked as everyone when he heard of my father's death. "I am so sorry. I expected to see him that December," he recalls sadly.

Haugland's wife Gerd appears from the kitchen with a platter of waffles and a coffee pot. "He was very upset," she says looking at her husband. "He is better now but he complains all the time," she adds playfully.

Haugland gives her a stern look and then turns to me. "We all looked up to your father," he says with a twinkle in his eyes.

"I remember he never had to study and yet he was always at the top of his class. He was very clever."

In recent years, Haugland tells me, my father would just show up in Lunde unannounced, driving one of his Citroëns. "I was always happy to see him," he says. "He always had something interesting to say."

Our conversation turns to Haugland and his poetry and his longtime working-class job with the railroad. I ask what he is working on now and he replies wistfully, "I am retired. I am too old to write." I suggest this isn't true, and encourage him to continue. At this his wife jumps in and agrees with me. Haugland looks pressured and uncomfortable. Nøve says politely it is late and time for us to leave.

On the drive back to Ulefoss I realize I have yet another snapshot of my father to put into the album that is his life, one that shows my father as a big fish in a small pond. It makes me wonder what happened to him when he immigrated to California and became one of many talented scientists from around the world. How did he feel? Was it a shock to go from the top of the mountain to the bottom? Did it affect his relationship with my brothers and me? And what role, if any, did it have in his own death?

3 5

Why was my father always building something? When I walk from room to room in the *lager* I feel like I am in an M.C. Escher etching with all paths leading to an image of my father with a hammer and saw in hand. I have very few memories of him relaxing.

I always thought the war had a lot to do with the way my father behaved. During some of my father's most formative years, his food was rationed, his movements restricted, and he secretly worked on radios in a tiny office under a constant threat of death. When the war was over and the restrictions lifted, my father responded by building obsessively and eating just about everything that was put on his plate. It makes sense.

Now after my evening with Haugland, I see the answer is more complicated. My father was well respected at the Livermore Lab but he was no longer a big fish in a small pond. The lab boasted some of the smartest people on the planet, and even though engineers like my dad were the ones who actually built something and made it work, it was the theoretical physicists who sat at the top of the food chain, commanding the most respect, and in many cases, the higher salaries.

My paternal great-grandfather, Karl Franz Christensen, at the family farm, circa 1930.

As the pond grew, so did my father's insecurities. The result was that he took up a lot of space, physically and psychically. I learned very young that there wasn't enough space or oxygen for both of us. Moving my bedroom into the bomb shelter was just one of the means I used to distance myself from my father and give myself breathing room. Even so, he never hit me. He never yelled at me. I don't remember him ever swearing at me. He spanked me once, but that was because I asked him to; my friends were all getting spanked and I felt left out. He spanked me and then said he would never do it again. I was put on probation instead.

After I left home and started having adventures of my own—putting real distance between us—my relationship with my father grew into one of mutual respect. But I was always vigilant about protecting my space, since he would quickly move in to fill it if I wasn't careful.

I am confident he saw things differently. This was brought home to me when I was in my mid-thirties and invited him to attend a one-day workshop on fathers and sons led by the poet Robert Bly. Bly traces his roots to Norway and I thought my father would enjoy listening to him, which he did. At one point during the day, I found my father leaning over into my seat, crowding me. It pushed a familiar button, but this time, in the spirit of the day, I voiced my irritation. My father listened, then put his arm around me: "But I was really only wanting to get closer to you." I was skeptical then, but now when I think back to that day I get a little sad because I believe he really meant it.

My wife did a similar dance with her strong-willed Spanish mother. Because of this, Rebecca and I share a common parenting philosophy that gives our girls a comfortable space to be themselves. I say this knowing full well that the day will come when they will articulate what they consider failings on our part. I can already hear them say, "You gave us too much space." Having children is a sure path to understanding and forgiving one's own parents. None of us is perfect.

I always thought it was important to remove myself from my father's shadow so I could find my own place in the world. But Hans...maybe he didn't need space the same way I did. Or maybe he needed it and that is why he did what he did. I don't know. I'm grasping at straws.

Rebecca and the girls are already asleep in the main house. I am in my makeshift office in the *verksted* looking at digitized copies of 16mm films my father shot in the '40s and early '50s. I've known about the films for years but never took the time to look closely at them until now. Some of the footage is in color but most of it is in black and white and all of it is priceless. Once I start, I can't stop watching and I lose all sense of time.

The earliest footage is from 1949 when my father sailed on a Norwegian freighter, the *M/S Hermund*. World War II was just four years in the past. The ship had no fixed route and carried dry goods from Norway and northern Europe to New York, timber from Vancouver to Los Angeles, spices from India to Italy, sugar from Cuba to Europe and even went as far south as Tasmania, for what I don't know. This was before modern containers so the ship typically was in port for a week or so as heavy-lift booms slowly unloaded the cargo of various sizes and weights. In the meantime the crew was free to explore; my father relished the opportunity and took a 16mm camera wherever he went.

There he is passing through the Suez and Panama Canals,

wandering around Bombay, and visiting pre-Castro Cuba. The shots in Havana are wonderful if only for the footage of vintage 1940s cars. He includes himself in many of the shots. He is thin and handsome, and his blond hair stands out like a beacon. To get these shots he must have mounted the camera on a tripod or handed it to a friend. In another reel my father is shown hitchhiking with a friend from a port in Italy to Norway for a home visit, passing through ruined European countryside in Belgium and Holland. Nøve told me that on his occasional visits home he'd bring hard-to-get fruits like oranges and bananas.

In one reel there are shots of him and the small crew at sea, in the mess, performing skits, and playing cards. There are a lot of smiles as the ship rocks. In the same reel is a shot of a huge shark thrashing madly on deck. In one scene the crew, including my father, poses with the shark, which is now hanging by its tail, its stomach slit open and the contents spilling on the deck. The final scene is my father walking along the deck waving one of the butchered fins at the camera as the ship sharply tilts back and forth on the rough sea.

I especially love the footage from Bombay. One gripping sequence shows a snake charmer with woven baskets filled with snakes and a tethered mongoose. In a close-up Dad captured a cobra, ready to strike, its head nearly filling the frame. There are shots of crowded wide streets and sidewalks filled with makeshift shelters. You can almost smell the poverty. Horse-drawn carriages weave through traffic filled with double-decked buses and ancient looking cars. A white bearded man wearing a Nehru-style hat shoves snuff up his nose.

Seeing the scenes from India reminds me of a story I heard directly from my dad when I was a boy.

"In Bombay," he told us with a twinkle in his eyes, "as I headed back to my ship after shore leave, a Sikh fortune teller grabbed me by the arm. He looked me in the eye and told me

My father and his parents in front of our house in Ulefoss, circa 1930.

I would marry a woman named Elizabeth, have three sons, and be very successful."

When he finished talking, Dad turned his palms upward as if to say, and look what happened. I always wondered what my father really thought about fortune telling. He was very much the rational scientist, but obviously he was also open to other ways of looking at the world.

Some of the most interesting footage is from 1951, just before Dad jumped ship in San Francisco. I know from Nøve that after two years at sea my father longed to settle down. "He briefly thought of moving to Tasmania," remembers Nøve, in one of many conversations about my father. "He loved it there; it reminded him of Norway. But then he decided it was just too far away from home."

San Francisco is another story. It is still far away from Norway, but at least it is in the same hemisphere. The first footage I see of the City by the Bay is the bow of a ship slipping under the Golden Gate Bridge. In the distance I see Coit Tower, just a stone's throw from where Rebecca and I and the girls live when we are in San Francisco. It's fun to see the car ferries carrying traffic between the East Bay and Marin County before the San Rafael Bridge was built.

And then suddenly there are shots of a beautiful brunette woman smiling broadly at the camera. I know who she is. She is my father's future wife. My mother. And her name? Elizabeth, of course, Elizabeth Ann Goodson to be exact. She is American and originally from the Midwest. By now, both my dad and mom are in their late twenties. Mom is working as a speech therapist at Kabat-Kaiser in Vallejo. They are introduced by a mutual friend one Saturday in March. Mom likes everything she sees in my father: his exotic life at sea, his accent, and his view of the world. And as for what my dad sees...well, she is beautiful, exotic, and...he has his prophesy.

Less than a week later they are married in Reno, Nevada. It's all captured on 16mm film. It's Friday, April 1, 1951 and there is a shot of my father and mother walking up the county clerk's steps, followed by another shot of them leaving, my father's arm draped affectionately over my mom's shoulder. Dad has a piece of paper in his hand. In a close-up I see it is the marriage certificate. Then there is a shot of my father leaving the Western Union office, where he has sent telegrams to his parents in Norway and to my mother's mom in Michigan. The news comes as a shock to both sides of the Atlantic. I have been told no one understood the hurry, or why my parents chose April Fool's day, of all days, to marry.

On that note, a new chapter in my father's life begins.

After a brief trip to Tijuana, Mexico, to straighten out my father's visa, my parents move to Fort Bragg, a coastal town in northern California, where my mother works as a waitress and my father at a lumber mill. They live in a tent on a rugged beach. There is footage of my father and mother eating charcoal-black potatoes taken directly from the open fire, and a precious shot of my mom running bravely toward the edge of the crashing surf and then turning suddenly around at the water's edge and running back up the beach. It's likely I am conceived at this very beach. At the end of the summer my parents move to a small apartment in the lower Haight area of San Francisco. Mom enrolls at San Francisco State and Dad at the University of California at Berkeley.

I am looking at shots of my mom cradling a newborn. She looks exhausted. It's me she is holding, born in San Francisco on June 3, 1952. The next frames jump forward in time and place and we are in Yosemite, camping. I'm still a tiny baby, and my father is poking a camera in my face, waking me from a nap. I am clearly not happy. The final footage is me as a toddler running naked toward the ocean and my mom running after me and scooping me up before I enter the Pacific.

That's it for the 16mm film; I've watched it all from beginning to end. I still have digitized versions of 8mm and Super 8mm film to look at, films from Livermore that include my two younger brothers. These films are from a part of my life I remember and experienced firsthand and I don't expect any surprises.

I pull back from the computer. Outside the window of the *verksted* it is pitch dark but I catch a faint glimmer of the moon reflecting off the surface of the river. I haven't seen anything in these 16mm films that foreshadows a man headed toward a tragic end. I see a young, handsome man, with a good eye for composition, full of life, leaving a record of what he saw and what he did. Was he successful, like the fortune teller predicted? I so desperately want to splice a different ending on the film that is my father's life. I want to give him a happy ending. Can I do that? Dad brought so many good things into the world. I only have to think about my daughters sleeping nearby for proof. He married a woman named Elizabeth, he had three sons, and except for a glitch at the end he was successful, very successful.

Fade to black.

Even when it is dark on our side of the river, the sun shines for another couple hours on the opposite shore. To get to the sunny side for an afternoon walk Rebecca and I drive our car down Lanna toward the Ulefoss Iron works, cross the old metal bridge, and then continue up a hill to the Ulefoss Hovedgaard. We park next to the tennis courts and start our hike. The Hovedgaard, literally "main farm," consists of a Napoleon-era mansion, a museum and an

English-style garden. The land was developed by the Aall family during the turn of the 19th century.

A few hundred yards from the manor, surrounded by majestic oaks, is a small greenhouse where my great-grandfather on my grandmother's side worked as a horticulturist. His name was Karl Franz Christensen and he was originally from western Sweden. Since he was a younger son with no inheritance to hold him back he moved to Norway seeking more opportunities. While developing a new variety of flax—one that would eventually win a gold metal award from the King himself—he spied a young maiden named Ingeborg walking by the greenhouse every day on her way home to her family's farm, Steinhaug. He courted and married her and moved to Steinhaug, where together they ran the farm and raised my grandmother, Anna Kristina (born 1902), and three boys, Ivar, Hening, and Alander.

Rebecca and I follow the same path that leads upriver toward the family farm, a path now still bathed in late afternoon sun. I can't help but think of Ingeborg and Karl Franz more than a hundred years ago walking this path hand-in-hand like Rebecca and I are doing now. I also can't help think of the days when I was a boy and Steinhaug was a working farm, with cows and many acres of tilled land. My brother Erik and I spent many hours in the musty, hay-filled barn, burrowing cave forts deep into the straw. We'd jump from the rafters into the soft piles below. We milked cows, used the outhouse, and even hand-pumped drinking water from the well. Today, my second cousin Oddvar, whose full-time job is with the local power company, runs the farm. There are no longer cows, although Oddvar still grows barley, hay, and grass for golf course seed on the side.

Everywhere I go I walk in the footsteps of my ancestors. If only they would walk in mine and tell me if I am headed in the right direction.

Steinhaug, the family farm.

It is cold and misty and there is snow on the ground. I just checked my messages and found that Hans called from Napa State Hospital. He sounded angry. He just reread a passage I wrote about Dad in one of my books, and he didn't agree with what I wrote about Dad's work at the Livermore lab. "Dad didn't know he was working on nuclear weapons," he said tightly. "You should set the record straight. Put something up on your web site."

Obviously our father knew what was going on. Nuclear weapon development was what the lab was mostly about in the '50s and '60s. Why is Hans defending Dad? December 11th— the anniversary of Dad's death—is only a few days away. Is there a connection? Hearing the edge in Hans' voice scares me. He is ill and I should be more understanding, but I also need to protect myself.

Today is the fourth anniversary of my father's death. I can't decide what to do; should I drive to Skien and shop for a new waffle iron, or visit my father's ashes at Tvara Lake? Instead, I sit at the kitchen table after Rebecca and the girls have left for school and sip espresso from my prized Pavoni and mull over the number four, looking for signs, significance, or guidance. After so many years associating with Kazz and Japanese culture, I respond to the number four with unease. The Japanese word for four shares the same sound, *shi*, with the word for death. But can't death also signify rebirth?

I decide to go to Skien. On the way, however, I change my mind and pull over at Meny, the local grocery store. I buy a bar of Firkløver—my father loved chocolate—and drive to Tvara. After breaking the bar into pieces, I toss them into the lake in the spot where I placed half of his ashes in the summer of 2005. That was the summer when Rebecca and I took our daughters to my recently acquired inheritance. (The other half of my father's ashes remains in California with my mother.)

We chose Tvara to place my father's ashes because it was always his favorite place, full of childhood memories. It is also where, nearly 30 years ago, in 1982, I shared with him the start of an amazing spiritual adventure, shortly after I learned of an ambitious Japanese project to save the world.

The project was the brainchild of an elderly Shinto priest who was affiliated with a shrine near Hiroshima. In 1973 the priest had had a horrific vision of end of the world—not surprising considering what happened in Hiroshima—and then another vision, one that showed a way to save the world from total destruction. In his vision, the priest was told by god to break an ancient Shinto sword, the "Sword of Heaven," into 108 pieces. The pieces were to be encased in stone, thereby becoming gods, or *kamis*, and then these were intended to be distributed around the world. The *kamis*, and prayers to the *kamis*, would create a network of peaceful energy that would push away bad spirits and stave off disaster.

My friend Kazz was one of the priest's students and he helped by carrying the gods to special locations around the world. Eventually, after I expressed interest in the project, Kazz sent me one of the *kamis*. At the time I was in Norway visiting my father, who had just been forced into retirement from the Livermore Lab.

It was my father who picked up the *kami* package from Japan at the post office in Ulefoss. It weighed several pounds, and the custom declaration contained the words, One Shinto God in large block letters. When he got home, he demanded an explanation from me. What the hell was I up to now? I told him what I knew about the project, thinking that my dad, who lived in a world of logic and rational thought, would reject it out of hand as a fantasy. Instead, he didn't say much of anything. When after a few days I still hadn't placed the kami, he suggested, seemingly out of the blue, that we place the stone god in the lake at Tvara together.

"It's surrounded by a national forest," he told me, "and fed by an underground spring. You said Shinto worships nature, so put it there."

That day we walked to Tvara, and then, on the rock where I am standing now, I tossed the kami into the lake while my father stood by taking pictures. With his blessing, I went on to help Kazz place Shinto gods all over the world, from Iceland to Berlin, from the Philippines to South Africa and the Amazon. I traveled to Japan and became more acquainted with Kazz and his teacher and Shinto. I was involved with the Sword project for six years; by the time I was finished the Berlin wall fell and the Cold War was over.

When I wrote a book documenting the project, *The Sword of Heaven*, I included a parallel story of my growing up in a bomb shelter and living with the fear of nuclear annihilation. Even back then I saw the connection between my father's World War II fears and my own. I acknowledged that the connection between the project and the end of the Cold War could very well have been coincidental, but I had no doubt that the project led to my own profound personal growth. It taught me how debilitating my own personal fears had become, and that the answer was to live with an open heart.

For awhile I was free of my old fears and I was happy. I met Rebecca and married her. We had two wonderful children and a pleasant life in San Francisco. But then my brother killed our father. My heart doesn't feel so open anymore. It is so hard for me to accept what Hans did with love and forgiveness. I wish I could. I want to be strong, but it is so difficult.

4 0

The river is layered with a soft but fast-moving mist. It is minus 15° C and sections along the edge of the river are frozen solid. At first it seems to me as if nothing is going on, that life along the river has ground to a halt, but then I take a moment to really look; only then do I see the reflection of the trees on the far side. I look some more and am rewarded by the sight of a duck popping to the surface after a long dive under the water, a succulent plant hanging from its beak.

Then I notice a faraway rock glowing in a shaft of weak sunlight. I look up at the pale blue sky, which is painted with a faint streak of soft white cloud. The effect is overwhelming. Beauty surrounds me, when just moments ago all was mundane and ordinary. All I have to do is slow down and look and the marvel of it all will be revealed.

My God, the river is so beautiful right now....

4 1

16 DECEMBER

The phone rings in the middle of the night but none of us hear it. When I go downstairs in the morning I check for calls that might have come in from the States overnight. Rebecca's stepfather Steve has left a message. Speaking slowly and deliberately, he asks us to call him

Tvara lake.

Rebecca's mom Francisca.

immediately. There is no answer at his home in Berkeley, so I call Rebecca's brother Michael in Los Angeles.

It is nearly midnight there but he answers the phone. He is sobbing as he tells me that Francisca, my mother-in-law, is dead.

There's so much to say about Francisca. As I mentioned earlier, she was a stunning beauty, with an infectious love of life. After living through two wars and the loss of her father when she was a baby, she left her native Spain in search of a better life in the U.S. (Her father, a Navy officer and engineer, was assassinated by a leftist death squad just before the beginning of the Spanish Civil War in 1936.)

In 1961, she married Michael Taggart, an American schoolteacher, and over the next few years gave birth to Rebecca and her younger brother Michael Jr. After five years of marriage, however, the couple divorced. Ten years later, Francisca, who worked as a Spanish teacher at Ojai Valley School, a private school in Ojai, California, married Berkeley realtor Steve Schneider. She moved north with him, eventually becoming a much-loved head librarian at a local library.

A few years ago, Francisca developed osteoporosis, and then breast cancer. She gracefully survived a mastectomy but soon after began to seem frail. She also developed clear signs of depression in the months before we left for Norway, displaying a melancholy attitude and despairing that no one needed her.

I might have recognized the warning signs of suicide, but I was actually more worried about Rebecca and the toll Francisca's health and behavior was taking on her. I knew Francisca as a woman of tremendous strength with a powerful life force, so what happened next catches me by surprise.

When Michael stops sobbing his first words are, "She did it. She jumped off the Golden Gate Bridge." My first reaction

is simple anger. Why? How could she do this? Her husband Steve loved her, Rebecca and Michael loved her, I loved her, our children loved her.

She had made previous attempts on her life, the first just a few weeks before our departure, but they had seemed more like cries for help than serious attempts. But now it hits me how much pain she must have been in, how desperate she must have been for escape from the black hole she had found herself in.

A witness had seen her at the bridge railing. The next moment she was gone, her wide-brimmed hat floating in the air. She was 72 years old.

We wait to tell the children about their *abuela*—grandmother in Spanish—until they come home from school. We sit on the floor in front of the fireplace and explain that *Abuela* had been in a lot of pain, but that she is now at peace.

Rebecca keeps her composure. Her grieving comes later, in private. We light candles in Francisca's memory and Ana weeps. "She understood me better than anyone," she says. Miranda is quiet, silently absorbing the difficult loss of yet another grandparent.

The fourth anniversary of my father's death has turned out not to be the sign of rebirth I'd hoped for, but a bringer of more tragedy and sadness.

4 2

It's the winter solstice, the shortest day of the year and officially the first day of winter. Today the sun rises at 9:19 a.m. and sets at 3:13 p.m., a full minute earlier than yesterday. The photo on the right was taken at noon, when the sun is at its highest. It seems as though the sun is farther away, but it's actually the low angle of the sun that makes it so faint at this time of year. Light has to travel farther through the atmosphere.

The sunlight is thin, and I feel thin too. The space between life and death seems almost tangible. I feel the ghosts of my ancestors everywhere, and now Francisca is with them as well. And yet I feel very alone and vulnerable; I take every comment from Rebecca or the outside world as criticism. I remind myself that this is what I wanted, I came here to dive deeply into myself, to explore the well. Ironically, when I try to write my feelings, very few words come out. It's as if I have dived past the very place where words are generated. Taking photos, on the other hand, is extremely satisfying. Through them I can communicate what I am truly feeling.

We observe the winter solstice at the home of Eric and Margrete Guerts-Lakin, a middle-aged couple who run an art gallery in the Gamle Apoteket, a lovely building on Lanna that was built in 1860 and that housed Norway's first rural pharmacy.

Margrete sets up a tree in the middle of the living room and adorns it with real candles. At one point in the evening our girls and the other children from the neighborhood hold hands, form a circle and dance around the lit tree, singing traditional Norwegian songs. It is a symbolic affirmation of the cycle of life, the return of the light, and the pushing

Noon, on the shortest day of the year.

away of the dark. Rebecca and I watch with mixed feelings. With the death of Rebecca's mom, all we can think of is once again protecting our girls from the full force of death and heartbreak. The effort it takes to maintain a busy and normal life uses every bit of our strength and energy.

We celebrate Christmas Eve with a service at the Flåbygd church, followed by dinner at Nøve and Sigbjørn's home in nearby Lunde. My cousin Halvor's eleven-year-old daughter Ingeborg, dressed up as the *julenissen* (Christmas elf), hands out presents.

Even though most Norwegians visit church on Christmas and Easter, few of them consider themselves particularly religious. This isn't to say that they aren't spiritual; I sense a powerful undercurrent that is grounded in the love of nature. My father's cousin Karl Steinhaug, for example, rarely goes to church, but when I ask him what his favorite activity is his normally stoic face lights up. He says he is happiest when he is alone in the middle of a forest, where he makes a fire and boils water. He sits next to the fire for hours, sipping fresh-brewed coffee, completely content.

I try his solitary ritual on my own the following week and it isn't long before the forest comes alive with visions of trolls, wood nymphs, and the Norse gods Odin and Thor dancing through my head. Death, which has surrounded us so much lately, seems far away.

On my way to the airport for a flight to San Francisco, I am attacked. It happens early in the morning in Oslo, when I cross the sidewalk from my hotel to catch the fast train to Gardemoen. A young man approaches demanding money in a slurred voice. He holds something in his pocket that he claims is a gun. I swing my hand luggage at him and catch the side of his face. Luckily, he runs away and I continue on to the station, shaken. On the train to the airport I tell some passengers what happened. They assume my assailant was a foreigner or an immigrant from the Middle East or Africa, but he wasn't; he spoke perfect Norwegian and was clearly born here. I am reminded that it is always so much easier to point a finger at others, and ignore the three fingers pointing back at you.

Update: On a Friday afternoon during the summer of 2011 we were in Norway again when my neighbor Leif yelled across the fence that there had just been a massive explosion in Oslo. I rushed to the Internet for news. First reports said it was likely a terrorist attack and al-Qaeda was immediately suspected. Shortly afterwards came reports of shootings at a summer camp on the small island of Utoeya. Again the focus was on terrorism from abroad.

As the world now knows, the bombing, which killed eight people, and the shootings, which killed 69 people, including a 14 year old, was the work of a single individual: 32-year-old Anders Breivik, a Norwegian Christian ultranationalist. Recently Breivik was diagnosed as paranoid schizophrenic and the experts who evaluated him describe him as a man "who finds himself in his own delusional universe, where all his thoughts and acts are governed by these delusions."

It all sounds too familiar to me.

The whole family has spent the last two weeks in California, attending the memorial service for Rebecca's mom Francisca, celebrating her vibrant and full life and mourning her death. We were happy to see our friends, but we were also a bit numb. It felt a bit unreal to be back, yet not really back. And it was very strange without *Abuela*.

We arrive back in Ulefoss to the largest snowstorm of the season. The electricity is out all along Lanna and it is pitch dark. We can't even drive into our driveway, the snow is piled up so high. One of our neighbors, Tore Halvorsen, kindly clears a path with his tractor. The electricity is soon back on and we build a roaring fire that quickly heats the house.

After spending a day clearing the courtyard, I settle back into a comfortable work routine of writing, editing, and printing photos in the *verksted*. The girls are back in school. Rebecca resumes her full-time Norwegian classes, which the Norwegian government provides at no cost. Her classmates include refugees from Africa and the Middle East who are staying at the nearby asylum center at Dagsrud.

My aunt often joins me in the *verksted*, driving down from Lunde with her acrylics and watercolors. With a fire crackling in the furnace and the river running silently past, it is a peaceful and precious time. Nøve is one of the last remaining relatives of my father's generation I can turn to with my questions about the family. And while she is very supportive of my search for meaning in her brother's death, she cautions me that there are no simple answers. In some cases, she says, there are no answers at all.

The girls and I are driving along the river, on our way to buy groceries. It's Saturday and quite cold, and we could easily spend the entire day indoors. Going shopping is mostly an excuse to get us out. As we pass the Gamle Apotek, Ana asks from the back seat, "What happens when we die?"

I'm surprised at her question and equally surprised at the ease with which the words come out of my mouth. I say that death is just a part of life, so it can't be bad. We'll know what happens soon enough when we get to the other side. In the rear view mirror I see Miranda nodding in agreement. Ana also seems content with my answer. We continue on our way to the store.

It is my hope that my children, who have already seen death close to home, will grow up without so much fear of it. You cannot fully live unless you can accept that death is an integral part of life. When we fear death, we fear life as well.

Today on my walk I take a photo of the Holla Church, a twelfth-century Viking ruin located on a hill overlooking Ulefoss. The tree in front of the church reminds me of *Yggdrasil*, the World Tree, or Tree of Fate, in Norse mythology. Legend holds that its branches extend all over the world and into the heavens. Three giant roots support the tree—one extending to hell, another to the frost giants, and the third to the land of humans. It is also said that three underground wells feed *Yggdrasil*: the Urda well, overseen by the three Goddesses of Fate; the Hvergelmer well, believed

The front of the family home on Lanna road. The building to the right with the Aaland name was my grandfather's furniture storefront.

to be the source of many rivers; and Mimer's well, the well of wisdom, guarded by Mimer himself, who is known as the wisest of all beings.

It's said that Odin, the most powerful Norse god, gave his right eye for a drink of the water from Mimer's well. What would I give? Must there always be a price to pay?

While driving past Lunde today, I see the most beautiful sight. A bright red fox with magnificent fur sits on the edge of the road staring at me. There is an old Norwegian children's song my father used to sing to me. It goes like this:

(Norwegian)	(English)
Mikkel Rev, satt og skrev,	*Mikkel Fox sat and wrote,*
på ei lita tavle	*On a little slate.*
Tavla sprakk,	*Chalkboard cracked,*
Mikkel skvatt,	*Mikkel jumped,*
opp i pappas flosshatt.	*up daddy's silk hat.*
Mikkel Rev, skrev et brev	*Mikkel Fox wrote a note*
sendte det til månen	*sent it to the moon*
Månen sa: "Hipp hurra"	*Moon said: "Hipp hurra"*
Sendte det til Afrika	*Sent it on to Africa*
Afrika, Afrika	*Africa, Africa*
ville ikke ha det	*would not have it*
Afrika, Afrika	*Africa, Africa*
sendte den tilbake	*sent it back*

Maybe because of my childhood association with this song

and its connection with my father, I have always loved foxes. At the moment I see the fox I am so stunned I almost crash the car. I take out my camera but it is too late. All that's left are prints by the road and along the frozen river.

Rebecca and I are headed to Skien, the birthplace of the playwright Henrik Ibsen and the largest nearby town, for our Friday "date night," which we try to do regularly to add spice to our otherwise practical day-to-day routines. It also happens to be the 17th anniversary of the day we met.

I didn't meet Rebecca until I was 39; she was 29. We met through a friend when I was on a photo assignment in Europe and she was vice-consul at the American embassy in Prague; it was love at first sight. Rebecca offered her couch when I couldn't find a hotel room. I never slept on the couch, though, and ended up subletting my house in San Francisco and moving in with her.

Rebecca met my parents in 1993 on a short visit to the Bay Area. My father was leaving for Norway and showed up at my home in San Francisco with a suitcase packed with boxes of nails and a gas-powered chain saw. He liked Rebecca immediately.

"She has a master's degree in chemistry! I like that," he confided to me, "Rational and beautiful."

Rebecca also took to him. "He's charming," she said. "But what does he have in his suitcase?"

I didn't even try to explain. It took a visit to Norway for Rebecca to understand. Not only did she see how expensive nails and chainsaws were, she saw my father's consuming and elaborate building projects firsthand.

My father saw a lot of potential in Rebecca and he was eager to give me romantic advice, something he had never done before. When I wrote and told him that I had bought Rebecca a fax machine so we could communicate better when we were apart he wrote back:

"Communication is very important in a relationship," he said, adding, "The first thing I bought your mother was a dishwasher."

He didn't explain how that improved communication between them but then again, he always saw things in a unique way.

Rebecca and I were married in 1994 in a redwood grove in St. Helena, California, with my friend Kazz conducting a sacred Shinto rite before we were officially wed. We had over 150 guests: Hans was there of course, along with my father, mother, Erik, and his girlfriend Bea. Nøve and Sigbjørn and my father's cousin Tulla flew in from Norway, dressed in traditional *bunad*. Rebecca's family and friends came from all over the country.

A snapshot of the weekend would reveal everyone getting along nicely and having a great time. You would see Francisca feeding Kazz raw oysters in the hot tub and my father cornering everyone he could to show off home video from Norway and Pi Pi. You would see Rebecca's father sobbing as he walked her to the grove of redwoods. You would see Hans riding his unicycle and talking about Jesus to anyone who would listen. You might guess that Hans is mentally ill, but you would never in your wildest imagination see him killing our father, nor would you imagine Francisca hurling herself off the Golden Gate Bridge.

Yes, there is always more to a picture than meets the eye.

February leads to March, which slowly brings an end to winter. The ice on the river recedes and patches of green appear on the sides of the road. My thoughts turn to another river that flows quietly through my blood. It is the river of my mother's family, which I can no longer ignore.

There is no one left from that side except my mother, who is an only child. When she was 13 her father, George Arthur Goodson, suffered a debilitating stroke and ended up in the veteran's hospital in Grand Rapids, Michigan. He died three years later. Her mother, an ambitious scientist and inventor, took a steady job as a lab technician in order to support both her mother and daughter.

When I was a child, my mother spoke infrequently about her father. When she did, I sensed an undercurrent of shame. From what little she said, I gathered he had been an alcoholic.

With little solid information to go on, I found myself blaming George Arthur for many of the ills in our family. When my brother Hans first exhibited signs of mental illness, I connected it to our maternal grandfather. I also attributed to him Erik's early struggles to hold a job and settle down. I wondered if malevolent ghosts had been passed down through him.

Recently, however, my mother told me that George Arthur had suffered his share of hardships. After a privileged youth that included a private boarding school and four years at Yale, George Arthur watched his father, a proud, wealthy businessman, lose everything in the Great Depression and later jump to his death from a building in Philadelphia. George Arthur's mother, who had Danish roots, suffered a stroke and died shortly after. My grandfather never graduated

My maternal grandfather, George Arthur Goodson and his mother Rene Olson.

from Yale, but took odd jobs selling ads for newspapers and teaching golf rather than playing it. Knowing all this, I now see him more sympathetically.

In one of those odd coincidences of life, my wife's father, Michael Taggart, was born in Grand Rapids. The Taggart family built summer cottages at Higgins Lake, three hours northeast of Grand Rapids, which they still use. During a recent family visit to the lake I drove to Grand Rapids and located the cemetery where George Arthur is buried.

I found the tombstone of George Arthur Goodson, Pvt.— Plot 7, Row 7, Grave 51—among those of the other World War I veterans. Earlier in the day I had searched for flowers but couldn't find any. I did, however, find a potted aloe plant and I placed it near the headstone and put my hand to the damp earth. I imagined George Arthur's body beneath me, its heart long stilled. I sensed a father's powerful love for his daughter, my mother, and it was that love I held onto. For the first time, Goodson, the good son, became real for me, more than just a one-dimensional character to blame for all our problems.

Could my mother have cleaned the waters simply by resolving her relationship with her father? At the very least she might have given me a clearer picture of him. I might have liked him instead of heaping blame on him. I might have seen him as I do now, flawed but very much human. I suspect George Arthur Goodson did selfishly indulge in earthly pleasures, and in doing so he may have muddied the family river. But I realize now that that nothing purifies better than the sunlight, and shadows are only a problem when we try to hide in them.

I said all this to George Arthur's grave and it made me even more determined to continue what I had started. I don't want to shove Hans' act into a closet and not deal with it; I want to counter that darkness with light so I don't pass any hidden baggage on to my children.

In my search for answers to my father's death, I leave no stone unturned. Was I somehow at fault? Did I do something wrong? What kind of older brother was I? I think my relationship with Hans was fairly typical. Like most brothers, Hans, Erik, and I engaged in petty sibling rivalry, just as I see my own daughters do. Was Hans competing with me for our father's love, his attention? Did I unconsciously drive a wedge between my dad and Hans, a wedge that drove him to kill our father in order to ultimately win the competition? Did he derive some kind of inspiration to "save the world" from own my work with Kazz on the Shinto project?

Survivor guilt is amazingly strong.

April Fools Day, and also my parents' wedding anniversary. If my father was alive, they'd have been married 58 years today, and that's no joke. In a desk drawer I find a yellowed paper with a typewritten poem from my mom. It is dated April First, 1989.

So here we are, you and I together

Thirty-eight years from our first ski trip

When we felt that our lives would weather

The unknown and uncontrollabale flips

That come with the long haul

You taught me to stride smoothly uphill

And when I fell I learned 'struggle and rise'

We skied across time and danced the quadrille

Our life is one: for us to eulogize

The best is yet to come

To: Kris, Min Mann, with love from Beth

I always knew my parents were bound by shared values and a strong commitment to family. They had many things in common; they liked to play chess and square dance and share the outdoors. But not sharing a common culture also created communication failures, and sometimes things were very stressful between them.

I imagine two very distinct rivers merging. In the confluence, the waters clash and spray and strive to maintain their uniqueness. I navigated the turbulence but sometimes I wonder if it was too much for Hans. Would it have helped if my parents were more in sync with each other? Could they have worked together better to pull him back from the abyss before it was too late?

In the face of so much turbulence, I long for still waters.

*Livermore, circa 1959. Left to right: Mom, Erik, Dad,
me, Grandma Goodson, Hans, Great-grandmother
Wyman, and Tante Ingeborg (visiting from Norway).*

Twenty years ago, my father built a dock and boathouse. This winter, the weight of the snow and ice piled high caused the entire structure to collapse into the river. In the spring I hire a local backhoe operator to pull the pieces out of the river, an operation that takes several hours. Everything my father built is substantial, so there are massive logs, cables, and steel plates to fish out of the river, finesse through the narrow space between buildings, and then finally into a dump truck parked on Lanna.

The boathouse is near the spot where my father nearly drowned as a child. When we were children he told us of the time he went out onto the frozen river in the winter, and the ice, unexpectedly thin, cracked. The next thing he remembered was being surrounded by warmth and going down a long hallway, feeling he was at peace. Then he woke up, brought back to life by a timely rescue. I've heard many other near-death experiences described exactly this way.

I wonder if Dad had a similar feeling on that fateful day when he took his last breath. I wonder what is at the end of the hallway.

The boathouse my father built,
before it collapsed.

A rare Mandarin duck on the Eidselva.

A few days after Easter I notice one of my neighbors, Trond Gisle Bjørsland, on the side of the road, tossing small pieces of bread into the river, so I walk up to join him. A flock of ducks appears, and the birds jostle for the crumbs. Suddenly, from the other side of the river, a brightly colored duck, the likes of which I have never seen before, crashes into the middle of the flock, which then flees.

It is a Mandarin, Trond explains. Normally found in China and Japan, it has migrated here in search of clean water and healthy forests. The lone bird is a phenomenon, and news crews from as far away as Oslo come to record its presence.

Trond was a good friend of my father's. He lives with Elizabeth A. Bjørsland, who inherited Aaheim, the old luxury hotel on Lanna, which long ago hosted the king and queen of Norway. The hotel is in disrepair now, to put it mildly, but Trond and Elizabeth have big hearts, and what they lack in terms of upkeep they more than make up for in good intentions.

When I tell Trond about my idea to combine the story of my father's death with photos and writings from the river, he is quickly philosophical. "You have to be sure and tell your readers," he says earnestly in English, "That every thought they have, every action they take, changes the world on a daily basis. Bring love and beauty into the world and the world responds. You told me that you are here in Norway to clean. Well, the cleaning starts in your mind. You have to take away negative thoughts and negative energy, take away feelings of guilt or anger. Observe them and then let them drift away. You don't want them to stick."

When he finishes, he leans back with a satisfied look. "We should talk more," he says. Although we see each other often, the moment for such talk passes and our conversations from then on are typical conversations between neighbors, concerned with the weather and other small-town topics. Nonetheless, I take what he said to heart and often think about it when I aim my camera lens at things of beauty, willing the beauty out to the rest of the world.

5 6

I have spent the last few hours scraping and sanding a window frame, preparing to paint. It's an old window and I'm removing 100 years of accumulated paint and grime. My fingers tingle from the vibration of the electric sander and my ears ring with the noise. I never thought of myself as handy, like my father and grandfather were, but this 116-year-old house demands constant maintenance so I don't have much choice.

I'm trying to enjoy the work but after a few minutes of sanding I want to grab my camera and head out to take photos or sit down at my computer to check email, read the news, or work on this book. In San Francisco I'd call Sean the handyman to do the job but there aren't any Sean's here. There are specialists—plumbers, carpenters, carpet layers—but they charge 600 kroner per hour, which is over $100. So I do almost everything myself, imagining my father and grandfather shaking their heads as I muddle my way through.

Spring explodes forth in Norway. One day the land is gray and barren and then, seemingly overnight, frozen streams thaw and water pours down wildflower-covered hills. We get nearly 17 hours of daylight now, and are seeing almost five extra minutes every day.

On this beautiful spring day, filled with the sweet smell of apple and cherry blossoms, I pack my camera equipment and drive upriver to the locks just past Lunde. Pulling off to the side of the road I am mesmerized by powerful streams of winter runoff spilling over the lock.

For one shot I set my camera shutter to 1/8000th of a second, which transforms every drop of water into a visible world of its own.

For the next shot something compels me to slow the shutter speed to 1/30th of a second. The result is a soft bur. It's the same water, the same river, and I'm standing in the same spot. The camera has just changed the way I see the world.

During this past winter I often felt separate and distinct from those around me, like a drop of water frozen at a very high speed. Now, on this warm spring day with the sun blazingly high overhead, I feel connected and indistinct. And at moments like this I know that time is continuous and unbroken. The past is as much a part of me as are the present and the future. At the same time, it does not control me. It informs me like a tail informs a dog but it does not drive me. I am my father's son, but I am also my daughters' father. Just as my father is also his father's son. We all make up the whole. I'm at the center of everything, distinct yet blurred.

It all depends on how you look at it.

Today is a day Norwegians all over the world celebrate. The 17th of May (Syttende Mai) is treated like the U.S. Fourth of July, with flags, parades, speeches, and dances—albeit without the military connotations or displays. Technically, however, the 17th of May isn't a day of independence, it is Constitution Day. It honors the landmark date in 1814 when Norway declared itself an independent country.

At the time, Denmark had ruled Norway for hundreds of years, but because Denmark had chosen the losing side in the Napoleonic Wars it had to cede Norway to Sweden. Inspired by the American Revolutionary war against Great Britain, Norway drafted its own constitution in a partially successful attempt to avoid Swedish rule. Even though Norway maintained its own parliament, judiciary, and executive powers, foreign relations were conducted by the Swedish King. The union between Sweden and Norway was officially dissolved in June 1905 when Norway adopted its own king and became a sovereign, independent country.

What put the fierce and independent Norwegians under the rule of Denmark and Sweden in the first place? Many social and economic factors contributed, but the main reason can be summed up in three words: the Black Death. The mid-fourteenth-century pandemic killed more than a third of the population of Norway over a two-year period, including most of the elite ruling class. Denmark, which was less damaged by the plague, stepped in to fill the void, and the rest is history.

Life is so fragile and fate so fickle. My ancestors have known this as well as anyone. And now so do I.

It's my birthday; I am 57 today. Rebecca and I celebrate with a late-night sauna and a quick dip in the still near-freezing river. Rebecca goes to the house to shower and prepare for bed while I sit by the side of the river nursing a Rignes, a Norwegian beer. Even though it's past 11 p.m., it is still light.

In the quiet of the almost-dark night, I listen to the river whispering to me. It's whispers words of encouragement, telling me that I am doing the right thing, telling me to stay on track, to keep digging for answers. In truth, I need the encouragement. I feel like I am stuck out on a limb, and the work I am doing is taking a toll. At times I feel totally toxic and exhausted, both mentally and physically. Part of me wants to stop what I'm doing and put my focus elsewhere, on another project. I want something that takes me far away from patricide, mental illness, and the job of cleaning up.

I want to push the Refresh button and just give all of us a new life. I ask myself, isn't that what I am doing? The river says Yes.

We need a new roof on the main house. The winter has been hard and water from the old tiles has seeped between the paint and the wood. In addition, the paint on the side of the house is peeling. Rebecca and I can paint on our own but the roof is a big job and we need professional help. We hire Kåre Bråthen, one of the most respected

My little Viking friend.

carpenters in town. He remembers my grandfather, another carpenter. He works with his son, Kjell Arne Bråthen, who also drives the bus that takes our girls to school.

Father and son are very efficient and the job takes them only a couple weeks. The painting, however, takes Rebecca and me over a month. Before we start we must scrape off the old paint, which takes forever. At first we scrape lightly and timidly. Then, urged on by more knowledgeable neighbors, we scrape harder. We peel away several layers of white paint and one layer of yellow paint before finally reaching bare wood. At this point, it only takes a week to apply a couple coats of new paint.

Come to think of it, the experience is not unlike solving a mystery. So much scraping before the answer is revealed.

6 1

Today is the summer solstice, the longest day of the year. Tomorrow marks the official first day of summer. The sun will rise at 3:54 a.m. and set at 10:44 p.m., giving us almost 19 hours of sunlight. Even at midnight the sky glows. Tomorrow we'll have ten seconds less daylight. Winter, though still far off, is on its way. We've experienced four distinct seasons here in Norway—a huge change from our life in California—and we're once again at summer. We aren't going back to the States until August but I take some time to reflect on where we are now.

Have we done what we set out to do? Norway is now firmly part of us as a family. My wife and girls speak Norwegian, and three of us have Norwegian passports. We've cleaned and painted and fixed up the property until it is quite comfortable.

My intense anger at my father for leaving a mess has receded. I feel closer to him than ever.

Do I understand why my brother did what he did? I have to answer: not yet.

6 2

We are getting rid of the last of my dad's Citroëns, a 1986 CX station wagon we have managed to keep running since my father's death. It still runs fine, but if we turn it in today we'll get 1500 kroner ($250) for recycling it, along with half the road tax we paid earlier this year, another 1500 kroner. If we wait until next year to turn it in, the car will have to go through another road inspection, which will cost us dearly in terms of maintenance. I stopped working on cars long ago and now rely on mechanics to do the dirty work.

It's a bittersweet moment. The car has served us well; even more, it is the last link with my father's passion for Citroëns, which started back in California in the '60s. For a while I shared his passion and owned a total of four Citroëns between my senior year of high school and my wedding day in 1994, when I sold my 1967 DS 21 Pallas to my dad.

It was time to move on then, and it is time to move on now.

After a luckless day of fishing in the mountains near Seljord—punctuated by a steady downpour—my cousin Halvor and I return to Ulefoss, an hour away. As I enter the *lager* to store my fishing equipment I see a small notebook lying just inside the door. It is deeply worn, and its stained pages are filled with beautiful cursive writing. The opening page contains the name Kristian Mikkelsen, Fiskhol, April 29, 1881. Kristian Mikkelsen was my great-grandfather, and Fiskhol was the name of the farm near where he was born.

I'd never seen the book before and I ask my daughter Ana about it. She confesses she found the notebook inside another book. She and a friend played school with it while Halvor and I fished.

Halvor tells me this is a *visebog*, a common schoolchild's songbook, and reminds me that Fiskhol is only a few kilometers from where we were fishing. It is also close to the headwaters of the river that eventually flows through our backyard.

This is what I learn about my family on my grandfather's side:

In the 19th century we were timber people, managing the forest that provided the logs that flowed down the Telemark canal past Ulefoss to Skien, where they were turned into lumber and sent to Paris and London and other faraway places. Some of the family, lured by the promise of more opportunity, left for America in the mid-1800s, settling mostly in Minnesota. My family was not alone; over 800,000 Norwegians immigrated to North America between 1825 and 1925.

Mountain life wasn't the life for Kristian Mikkelsen, who

My paternal great
grandfather, Kristian
Mikkelsen, lies in state in
the courtyard of our family
home. My grandfather
and his two sisters pay their
respects. Mikkelsen's songbook
(insert).

was born in 1863. He migrated downstream, ending up in the town of Ulefoss, which boasted an iron works and burgeoning commerce. In 1892, with his wife, a local girl named Ingeborg Nyhus, he built a house on the plot of land known as "Aaland." For income, he managed a nearby supply cooperative. Over the next few years, they birthed two daughters and a son, my grandfather.

Ingeborg Nyhus died in 1912 at the age of 48. Kristian Mikkelsen died in 1931, at the age of 67. His body lay in state in the courtyard between the house and the *verksted*. I have a photo of Kristian Mikkelsen's casket in the courtyard, under a pile of flowers, with my grandfather and his two sisters standing nearby, heads bowed.

I imagine Kristian Mikkelsen as a romantic figure, inclined more toward poetry and daydreaming than logging or other physical pursuits. I imagine this partly because of things my father said about him, but also because of the *visebog*. There were many entries, including the one I've translated here.

Ei Telemarkens jente, saa fager og fin

i Hujen sin Guten ho gjømmer.

Ho blømmer som soli, naar Vaarsoli sjin,

og Hugnad fraa hennar de fløimer.

Dæ æ injo Møikjering skulle du det sjaa,

i syttende aare ho æ fyste naa,

men endaa om hennar dei drøimer.

A beautiful girl from Telemark

Hides her thoughts of her lover.

She blossoms when the spring sun shines,

And joy flows from her.

This is not an old-unmarried-woman,

She is seventeen years old,

And boys around her dream.

Although it's a small book it seems very large to me, and opening and reading it leads me to another world. I imagine my great-grandfather sitting next to a clear mountain stream, his young face turned to the sky, hand and pencil poised above paper, struggling to pour his feelings into a poem. As he does this, I sit side-by-side with him and the past.

I am on top of a small hill near our house. An occasional hiker makes a small impression on the landscape but I am otherwise alone, surrounded only by rocks and trees and water. In the midst of so much open space, I feel room to grow and be happy. I feel as much a part of the earth as Leif's cherries are part of his tree.

Today is Hans' 51st birthday. Even though I don't understand the reason for his actions, on a beautiful day like this it is easy for me to feel at peace with the world. In my expansive mood I am able to feel compassion as well as love for my brother Hans. He has his delusions and an uncertain future, I have my health and my freedom. I don't have closure, but I am closer.

The wild raspberries and blueberries are at their peak. I mix and mash the ripe summer fruit with a little sugar and then spread the jam on homemade waffles. Delicious. There is no such thing as just one bite.

We fly back to San Francisco in a week. We've had a great year but it's time to go back. Mom turns 86 in September and I feel the need to be closer to her. Ana is also ready to return home. Even though she's made good friends here in Norway, she misses her San Francisco friends. Miranda and Rebecca are more reluctant to leave—Miranda has bonded with a special group of girls and Rebecca isn't entirely ready to give up her daily walks in the Norwegian woods and return to the urban jungle—but they also know that it's time to go. Norway is very much part of our life, however, and we'll be back. The river isn't going anywhere.

Our flight touches down at San Francisco airport on a cool summer evening. Peering through the oval windows of the plane, we look for familiar landmarks and marvel at the delicate fingers of fog flowing over the coastal mountains. I am so excited to be back I am not aware that I am slowly bleeding to death. Literally.

We collect our bags and pile into two cabs, Rebecca and Miranda in one, Ana and I, along with all of our luggage, in another. It's a 30-minute drive to our home in North Beach.

Our Swiss family renters have moved back to Switzerland, so our apartment is vacant. Everything is in order, and after a light supper we prepare for bed and sleep soundly, lulled by the gentle moans of foghorns and the muffled barks of sea lions.

The next day is a blur, and I notice how quickly we are slipping back into our San Francisco life. I am unusually tired, but I blame my fatigue on jet lag and the effort of moving the family halfway across the world. The following morning I awake from a vivid and shocking dream in which the floor around the bed is covered in blood. I shake off the feeling of horror and get up, only to collapse while struggling up the flight of stairs to our kitchen. Rebecca calls the hospital, then rushes me to the ER.

Doctors tell Rebecca I am close to death. I have lost over a third of my blood through a gaping ulcer in my stomach lining. As I slip in and out of a painless haze I ask myself, what have I done? Why is this happening to me? Have I tried too hard to find answers to my father's death? Is this the price I have to pay for my pursuit of an answer? Is this simply the end?

Obviously it's not. I'm given three blood transfusions and when I am stable doctors perform an endoscopy and close the stomach wound with three staples. They test for H. pylori, the bacteria associated with ulcers. When the results come back negative, they place much of the blame on ibuprofen, the painkiller I've been taking off and on for the past few years for muscle cramps. I'm convinced, however, that the main issue is stress; I have been in rough waters and it's not surprising I am banged up.

It takes me months to generate enough new red blood cells to get back to full strength. I spend much of the time in front of the computer, going over what I have learned about my family, writing and trying to shed light on the darkness that has befallen us. Doing this gives me a sense of control, something I have been sorely lacking.

My mother, who is living comfortably in her small apartment in Livermore, also reads my attempts to document our family history. Prompted by my comments about her father, she has taken out her albums and pulled out photos of her father and family. She shows me a painting of Chief Joseph Brant, the Mohawk leader who sided with the British during the American Revolutionary War, and tells me we are directly related to him. Brant's youngest daughter, born in 1794, was also named Elizabeth, the same as my mother. I don't know why she never told me all this before. For the first time, my mom fleshes out George Arthur Goodson and puts his life on the table for me to see. I sense she is exploring her relationship to her father, and her family, anew. I welcome the change.

I have no doubt my investigation is a positive force. My research and my time on the river have connected me with my ancestors, my father, and myself. Through my photography I have also connected to something beyond words, to nature and beauty. As a detective, however, I still haven't found a satisfying explanation for my brother's violent act.

After two years of serious health issues that began when we returned from Norway, I am fit. First there was the bleeding ulcer, and then exactly a year later I was treated with two stents to open a partially blocked coronary artery. Six months later, the medicine I took for the heart condition led to another stomach ulcer. Now that I feel stronger I am finally ready to confront Hans directly.

He is now at Gladman Memorial, a small mental health rehabilitation center in Oakland, just across the bay from me. He was transferred here from the Napa State Hospital just before we returned from our year in Norway in 2009. He's been declared unfit for trial, although he insists on proceeding. As long as Hans says he is perfectly sane and not guilty he'll remain in legal limbo.

As a reward for good behavior, Hans is allowed to accompany a family member offsite for three hours. Today we are at Peet's Coffee in Oakland, just a few minutes drive from Gladman. I buy him a cappuccino and as he sips the frothy caffeinated drink, he becomes more lucid than usual. He asks about my daughters, genuinely interested in how his nieces are doing. He asks about Rebecca. He is concerned about my ulcer and my heart. Like me, he also has high cholesterol—it must be hereditary—and is on statins. He thoughtfully suggests more natural ways for me to lower my cholesterol.

Then he wonders if our brother Erik will ever visit, or even talk with him.

"He's angry at you," I say. "He can't let Dad go."

Hans nods understandingly.

"It might help if you said you were sorry," I say. "He has nightmares about what happened."

Hans pauses then says, "I am sorry. I'm sorry I did what I had to do."

Now I'm quiet. This is not an acceptable apology, not for me nor, I'm sure, for Erik. Hans sees what he did as a sacrifice to God, I see it as murder.

"You know I loved Dad," he continues.

It takes everything I have to remain quiet and let him talk. I know many of the details from the police report but now

Hans fills in the blanks. I will myself to listen to every word he says and face the horror of that morning straight on. It is one of the hardest things I have ever done in my life.

Hans spares no details. He recounts the morning seven years ago when he woke up and made his decision to "sacrifice" Dad. He had received many signs, going back several weeks. Passages in the Bible leaped out at him. He describes our father's reaction when he put the t-shirt over his mouth.

"Dad struggled, but then he looked me in the eye and said, 'Are you trying to kill me?'"

What was our father thinking? What was it like to realize that his own son, his own flesh and blood, literally held his life in his hands? I feel nauseated at the thought.

Hans continues, "I told him God told me to do it. I told him it will bring peace to the world." Hans is quiet for a moment before he continues. "Later I cried. But then I was ok. I did what I had to do. I've seen Dad in dreams. He forgives me. He understands."

Should I challenge him or just let him live with his delusions? I am torn. He finishes his coffee. I decide I have had enough. I won't say anything and I can't listen anymore. It is too painful. I suggest we go.

We drive the short distance from Peet's back to Gladman. I struggle to make small talk about the weather, football, anything to divert the conversation and my thoughts from our earlier conversation. I feel like I am in a bad dream, and I desperately want to wake up and put an end to it. Back at the Gladman parking lot I hand Hans a package of chocolate I brought back from Norway. It's a tradition in our family. Whoever goes to Norway brings back chocolate for the others.

"Thanks," he says, obviously thrilled with my gift. Then he adds softly, "You know if Dad wasn't dead, you wouldn't have Norway."

He says this so softly at first I think I've misunderstood him.
But then he adds, "And your daughters and Rebecca wouldn't
have it either."

Now I am torn between hitting him and pushing him out of
the car.

"You have any idea how hard things are?" I hiss, years of
pent-up rage emerging. "How difficult the last seven years
have been?"

He recoils at the harshness of my voice. I see how fragile he
really is, but I am on roll and I can't stop.

"You think my ulcer, my heart...you think my problems just
came out of the blue? And Rebecca and the girls...they would
rather have *Bestefar* alive."

I immediately wish I could take back my words. I want to
stay on the high road, but I'm sinking. Part of the problem
is I know he is right. If Dad had lived, eventually I would
have inherited the family property, but how old would I
have been? How old would my daughters have been? Would
they have developed the connection with Norway they have
now? Would I even have found out about my Norwegian
citizenship?

"I can never accept what you did," I say finally. "No matter
the outcome, it was wrong."

I'm walking a thin line. Hans has built a construct that
protects him from facing the reality of what he has done. The
walls are very thick. What would the consequence be if they
broke? I keep pressing him. This is about me, not him.

"I know God told you what to do. But that is not the God I
know. It's not the God I respect. God doesn't tell people to
kill others. You have to stop listening to the voices that tell

you otherwise."

"I don't hear voices," he mumbles, and then says something about Abraham and the Bible and God telling Abraham to sacrifice his only son.

"That's the Old Testament!" I shoot back. "You always talk about Jesus. He's your guy. He preached love."

Hans looks blankly at me and suddenly everything becomes clear. I am talking past him. Nothing I say sticks, just like nothing he says sticks to me. We exist in parallel universes and it is futile to argue. I have to let it go.

"Hans," I say quietly, "he was our father."

I can see Hans is upset. I know he desperately wants me to understand his side of the story. He wants me to know he loved Dad and that he acted for everyone's sake. I know he wants me to believe he did it to save the world. And I think he realizes at this moment that I can never understand. He quietly reaches for the door and prepares to leave.

I don't want to end our visit this way. I am not angry anymore. I am just sad, very sad. Before he closes the door, I tell Hans I love him and I'll see him again soon. He nods and then turns and walks back to Gladman, where a receptionist is waiting for him with the door open.

My father and Tante Ingeborg, circa 1932.

Mom died peacefully this morning, eight years after Dad's violent death and a week shy of her 89th birthday. Her heart valve, the one that was supposed to fail six years ago, finally gave out and her lungs filled with fluid, effectively drowning her while she was in a coma. Even though she died peacefully with no pain, there was plenty of drama surrounding her death.

A month earlier, in July, she was relatively strong, and regularly driving herself to the theatre, her weekly bridge match, and to Livermore-Amador Symphony Association meetings. I was in Norway for the summer with Rebecca and the girls, as usual. At the beginning of August my brother Erik called to say Mom had had a stroke and was under observation at Kaiser Hospital in Walnut Creek. He told me there was no reason to change our August 16th return date. She was stable, he said and she would be moved to Stonebrook Health Care in Concord for therapy and observation.

On August 11th, Rebecca flew back to San Francisco alone. She had a new job teaching science at Gateway High and was required to be home earlier than the girls and me.

On Wednesday morning, the day the girls and I planned to leave Ulefoss for the airport, I woke up and right away knew we had a big problem. I was bleeding internally again. By then, I was well aware of the signs. Like with my previous ulcers, I didn't feel pain, but I was unusually tired and there was obviously old blood in my stool. I had enough energy to slam my fist against the bathroom wall in frustration and then call Uncle Sigbjørn. He drove me to the local clinic in nearby Lunde where the German doctor confirmed what I already knew. She prescribed a proton pump inhibitor (PPI) to calm my stomach and told me I should go to the hospital in Oslo for a more thorough check up before taking the long flight back to San Francisco.

That evening, after we took the train to my cousin Bjørn Gregert's house in Bærum, an Oslo suburb, a young Norwegian doctor at the Bærum hospital advised me not to fly until the bleeding stops.

"It is a slow bleed," he said, "but if it opens up on the plane it could be disastrous."

He agreed to let me drop my girls off at the airport in the morning, but he wanted me to check into the hospital afterwards, where I could be observed and intravenously fed a strong antacid.

By the time I got to the hospital after seeing the girls off, I was worn out. Lying in the hospital bed, surrounded by attentive Swedish and Danish nurses, I Skyped Rebecca and told her the girls are on their way and not to worry, that I was well taken care of. Lying in the next hospital bed was a fit-looking older businessman who just learned that his cancer had spread and he had only a few months left to live. He couldn't believe this was happening to him. I only had an ulcer and talking with him made me feel incredibly lucky.

I didn't feel so lucky on Saturday evening when I got a Skype call from Rebecca. "Beth just took a turn for the worse," she says "Her heart valve is failing quickly. She is alive, but she can't even get out of bed she is so weak. It's not good. Take care of yourself, but try and get home as quickly as possible."

That evening I pleaded with the doctor to release me from the hospital, but he refused. On Sunday morning, my blood levels were finally stable and the doctor reluctantly gave me the green light to fly. As he filled out the release forms, I quickly booked a Lufthansa flight to San Francisco via

Munich for the next morning, then gathered my things and waited for my cousin Bjørn Gregert to pick me up.

On Monday morning I was in the Oslo airport lounge waiting for my flight when I got an urgent call from my brother. It was Sunday night for him.

"Mom just went into a coma," he said, choking back a sob. "It's probably too late for you to say goodbye."

A nerve-wracking 14 hours later, Rebecca picked me up at SFO. "She is still alive," she said. As we drove to the Kaiser hospital in Antioch she explained, "They have waited to remove the respirator until you got here, but then it will be all over. I am so sorry."

When we arrived Erik and his girlfriend Bea were by Mom's side. Erik got up and grabbed the Norwegian chocolate bar I was clutching in my hand and placed it on Mom's chest. "This will help," he said confidently. "This will bring her back." I could barely see Mom's face. It was covered with a mask and she was breathing only by the grace of the machine, which hissed and wheezed on a regular beat. I leaned over and found a place on her forehead to plant a kiss. My tears dropped on the hard plastic tube leading down her throat.

A nurse told us they are going to wait until the morning to unplug the respirator. She shook her head when I asked what would happen then. She didn't know. Rebecca took my arm and said softly, "It will be all over." Hearing this, Erik gave her a hard stare and then said harshly, "No, you are wrong. It's not over. She will be ok. I know it."

Rebecca was quick to answer. "Erik, face reality!"

I was too jetlagged, too tired, too drained to step between my wife and Erik. They had both been with Mom for the last week and obviously it's been stressful for both of them. None of us took Mom's demise calmly. We sat in silence for

My maternal great grandfather,
George Arthur Goodson Sr..
Circa 1925.

another hour or so. Around 11 p.m., when it was clear there was nothing left for us to do we left the hospital. As we left, I confirmed with the nurse they wouldn't do anything until after I arrived the next morning.

When I arrived I was in for a shock. They have removed the respirator without waiting for me. Mom was propped up in bed with a smile on her face. She had trouble talking, but after saying hi, her first words to me were, "Is this the end of the book?"

What book? I was confused. She is a writer. Was she talking about the book of her life? Or did she mean this book, the one I am writing about our family? It didn't matter. I was thrilled she was alive. Then Mom grabbed my arm and whispered so quietly I could barely hear her. "Next time," she said urgently, "Next time, let me go."

When I reached my brother Erik on the phone and gave him the good news, he cried out joyfully "I told you! She wasn't going to leave until she got the chocolate! Rebecca was so wrong." I didn't say this to my brother, but I preferred to think she came back from the coma to say goodbye to me.

Mom lived another week and a half. She moved back to her old room at Stonebrook and received a steady stream of visitors who were just as amazed at her recovery as we were. Our girls, Rebecca, and I made several trips across the Bay to visit her. We even brought Hans, who got special permission to leave Gladman for the afternoon. Even when she talked about going home to Livermore I could see she knew the end was near. When I turned my video camera on her she seized the opportunity and turned the recording into a goodbye to all her friends. She ended with "I hope to see all of you again sometime soon. I love you all."

Once again it was Erik who called with the bad news. Mom's lungs had filled with fluid and she was in a coma again. They had moved her to the ER and when I arrived she was hooked up to a respirator. This was not what she wanted; she made that perfectly clear last time. When I protested, the doctors found her "Do not resuscitate" directive in the computer and unhooked her. She lived through the day. That evening, before she died, I stroked her face and marveled at how soft her skin was and how slight her body had become. She was so ready to go.

We hold Mom's service today at Callaghan's mortuary in Livermore, the same location where we held Dad's service in 2004. It is her birthday and Mom would have been happy to see that over 100 people show up, matching the number who showed up for Dad's service. My parents were always competitive with each other.

Hans is at Mom's service with an escort from Gladman. He is quiet and subdued, yet mingles easily with the crowd. If anyone is nervous around him they don't tell me. I think most people who know our family take it for granted that he is here, especially considering how close he was to Mom.

After we project Mom's videotaped goodbye several people stand up and eulogize her. Then Hans gets up and sings "Scarborough Fair." His hands shake from the antipsychotic medicine as he sings the first lines, "Are you going to Scarborough Fair? Parsley, sage, rosemary, and thyme." He sings beautifully, like an angel. By the last line, "Then she'll be a true love of mine," there isn't a dry eye in the room, including my own.

As he slowly shuffles back to his seat it is hard to imagine this person killing our father eight years ago. His love for Mom has touched my heart and revealed a goodness inside him that has been there all along. Our mother, whose spirit is surely smiling right now, already knew that and that is why she was so quick to forgive. After the service is over Erik goes up to Hans and gives him a hug. It is the first contact my two younger brothers have had since Dad died. We have come a long way.

PART 3

The way you help heal
the world is you start with
your own family.
—Mother Theresa

My mother's death, along with Hans' touching performance at her memorial, marks a turning point in my search for answers to my father's death. I have been exploring numerous psychological factors that may underlie what Hans did, now I am ready to move on. Hans committed an evil act that will haunt me for the rest of my life, but he is not fundamentally evil. He was mentally ill and continues to be so. The more important question for me now is what can I do next to help make things right for myself and my family?

The answer starts with another email from Kazz. He is finally healthy and ready to make the pilgrimage to Mt. Kailash, the holy mountain in Tibet. He writes:

> *Mikkel. I decide to go to Mt. Kailash from Nepal. This year is special for me. I will go July. I want to know, you will come or not? If you come, we can use same room and tent. So please tell me. I will book soon. love Kazz*

This pilgrimage—an ancient spiritual tradition inspired by magical thinking—feels right. I am not a Buddhist, nor a Hindu, Jan, Bon, or Shintoist, but I can use a pilgrimage to Mount Kailash as a way to honor my father, my mother, and my ancestors. It is a way to atone for my brother's act and bring balance back to my life. And what better companion than my dear friend who has guided me on my path to understanding?

It is perfect timing: My daughters are older and more independent, Rebecca is very supportive. In July we will be in Norway and it will be easy to fly to Asia from Europe. My mom has left me some money, which I can use to pay for the trip. I ask myself, am I healthy enough? I will not let fear hold me back.

The mountain is tucked away in a remote western corner of Tibet and it takes days of grueling overland travel to even get there. The path around the mountain is a rugged 52 km (32 mi) and takes three long days to walk. The average altitude in Tibet is over 15,000 feet and the pass we will hike over is nearly 19,000 feet. Dozens of pilgrims die every year from altitude sickness.

It is a chance I am prepared to take. The mountain is the geographic source of the four major rivers of the Indian subcontinent, and I can imagine it as the spiritual headwaters of my own personal river. What a fitting place to seek clarity and peace of mind. I write back and tell Kazz to count me in.

7 1

13 JULY 2013

It is 5:02 in the morning and I am on my way, taking a train to the Oslo airport. My compartment is full of sleeping passengers, many of whom have been on the train all night. Plastic bottles of Coke and crumpled bags of chips litter the aisles. The few passengers who are awake stare blankly at brightly lit laptop screens. The summer sun has been up a long time, and I gaze through the large window at the steady progression of evergreens, frequently punctuated by flashes of lake or river, or sparking masses of granite. Unlike the messy train, the Norwegian landscape is beautiful and unspoiled.

Telemark, Norway.

Even though Rebecca and our daughters are staying in Ulefoss, I am not alone. I carry with me the dead, literally and figuratively. In my bag are some of my parents' ashes, as well as proxies for my long-dead grandparents. The last time I called a family meeting, things didn't go the way I expected. My father didn't even show up. Since then I have gotten to know my ancestors better. In Tibet, I hope to get some kind of conclusion from them, an indication that I have done what I need to and can move on.

I lean back in my seat and scribble words in my notebook. From now on everything I do or think is touched with significance. It's hard to believe it, but this is really happening. In my notebook I write, "I am no longer planning. I'm doing."

7 2

The eight-hour flight from Oslo to Doha is smooth and uneventful. After a five-hour layover, I am back in the air for the five-hour flight to Kathmandu. As the sun rises we start our steep descent into the Kathmandu valley. Apologizing, I lean over the woman next to me, snapping photos of the towering, white-capped Himalayas to the north and the crowded, smog-filled valley below.

When I am done I turn to the woman, a young nurse from Virginia. She tells me she will volunteer at a Nepalese orphanage. The orphans are young children who have lost their parents to war, disease, or natural disasters. She doesn't know what to expect and is excited and nervous at the same time. We are landing so our conversation is brief but long enough to make me question my own purpose here.

As we leave the plane, I say goodbye to the nurse. I tell her I admire what she is doing and wish her luck. Although I don't say it, I also envy her; her mission here is clearly defined, unlike mine. How will I know if I succeed? Must Hans suddenly be cured of schizophrenia and understand the consequences of what he did? Must my girls live unencumbered lives, without the burden of the past? Must I be happy? The questions demand answers I cannot easily give.

I am asleep in my hotel room in Thamel, a touristy district in the center of Kathmandu, when I hear a soft knock at the door. It is Kazz, arriving from Japan. He is an experienced traveler and knows this part of the world well. When he couldn't find the travel agent who arranged our trip—the one who met me at the airport and helped me get to our hotel—he jumped into a taxi and navigated here on his own.

It's been nearly 20 years since I last saw him. He looks lean and fit. He turns 61 next week, and hints of gray hair are the only testimony to the passing of time. We hug and then act as if we just saw each other yesterday. Like me, he is here on a mission. He carries holy Shinto artifacts in his suitcase and already has a place in mind at the base of Mt. Kailash to bury them. I am not sure where I will conduct my family meeting, but I hope I will know when the time and place are right.

We have been waiting four days in Kathmandu for our permit to enter Tibet. We are impatient to leave but I've also enjoyed hanging out here with Kazz. He has been to Nepal several times and is the perfect guide to the city. Everywhere I go I want to stop and take a photograph and

Kazz encourages me. My eyes and camera can't get enough of the constantly changing stage of people, cars, bikes, and rickshaws. In the middle of this teeming, sometimes dangerous, commotion Kazz has my back.

This afternoon, at a café overlooking the *Boudhanath Stupa,* the largest Tibetan sacred monument in the world, Kazz asks me about my brother. He wants to know how Hans is doing.

"Pretty well," I say. "I see him regularly. By killing our father, he has what he needed most, top-notch medical care and a supportive environment. He claims he did it to save the world, but he ended up saving himself."

We sip cups of steaming hot honey, ginger, and lemon tea, which we've quickly dubbed "magic tea" because it tastes so good.

"And what about the family river?" Kazz asks. "Did you find any bad karma upstream?"

"Not really," I reply. "I discovered a lot of denial and fear on both my mother's and father's side. That counts for something. But no smoking gun, nothing to be ashamed of." And, after a moment I add, "I am more focused now on cleaning the mess my brother left behind."

"That is why you are here," Kazz says knowingly. I pick up my camera from the table and nod in agreement.

We get up to leave. Kazz needs a ceremonial robe for the Shinto ceremony he will perform at Mt. Kailash so I follow him as he gracefully navigates the twisted, crowded streets until we arrive in front of a small clothing shop. Inside he haggles with the owner over the price of a white Nehru-style jacket.

"This will do," he says as we leave the shop, jacket in hand. A visibly happy storekeeper beams behind us.

Kazz with cow and pigeons in Kathmandu.

When we arrive back at our hotel our Nepalese travel agent is waiting with good news. Our permit to enter Tibet has finally come through from the Chinese government. The first time I applied I submitted my Norwegian passport and my visa was denied. Evidently the Chinese are still angry with Norway for giving the Nobel Peace Prize to the Dalai Lama, and then to the Chinese dissident Liu Xiaobo. Ironically, it is my American passport that comes back with the visa.

7 4

We have started. It's only 114 kilometers (71 miles) between Kathmandu and the border of Tibet via the Araniko Highway, but these are some of the toughest kilometers I have ever traveled. It is the main road between the two countries, but most of it is dirt, and often impassable because of rockslides, deep mud, or political strife.

Six hours later, in the middle of Kodari, the border town on the Nepalese side, we find huge boulders blocking the dirt road. We have to abandon our car and walk the last couple kilometers to the Friendship Bridge that connects Nepal and Tibet. It begins to rain. Our Nepalese travel agent, who has accompanied us from Kathmandu, hires two porters to carry our luggage. Kazz brought a hard-sided suitcase with no wheels or straps. His porter grimaces as he holds an umbrella awkwardly in one hand and lugs the suitcase in the other. We are surrounded by throngs of Indian pilgrims who are also on their way to Tibet and Mt. Kailash. As the rain comes down harder, everyone looks miserable, even though no one is complaining.

At the Chinese border crossing we say goodbye to our Nepalese agent and porters; Dorji, a Chinese-approved guide, and Sitar, our driver, take over. Both are middle-aged Tibetans and while Sitar does not speak much English, Dorji's is good. He used to be a Tibetan priest, and knows the country intimately. Although he lives in faraway Lhasa, he has circumnavigated Mt. Kailash 114 times.

When Dorji hears that Kazz has been here before, I see the two of them exchange knowing glances. It is as if they are members of an elite club, and no further words are necessary. With Dorji leading the way, we pass easily through Chinese passport control. The security guards seem mostly interested in whether or not we are carrying illegal photos of the Dalai Lama. Soon we are back on the road, continuing the three-day drive west to Mt. Kailash.

We are in Nyalam, a one-street town dominated by simple hostels full of pilgrims on their way to Mt. Kailash. Yesterday we climbed from Kodari's 2,515 meters to Nyalam's 3,750 meters in just 33 kilometers (21 miles). We are scheduled to stay here an extra day to acclimate to the sudden change in elevation.

It is a good thing we stopped, as I am feeling the first symptoms of altitude sickness. Last night I slept poorly, with a throbbing headache, wondering obsessively why I came and what was I doing? Waves of doubt kept me company most of the night.

At first I was reluctant to take Diamox, the medicine prescribed by my doctor to prevent altitude sickness. I am already taking prescription drugs for my stomach and heart conditions and I don't want to add any more to the

Western Tibet.

list. I change my mind in the morning when a doctor from Los Angeles who is traveling with one of the Hindu groups assures me that Diamox simply accelerates the body's natural acclimation to altitude, with few or no side effects.

Within hours of popping my first pill I feel better, my doubts replaced by determination and eagerness to continue our journey.

My headache is completely gone and we are on the road again. Kazz, who's also taking Diamox, is in a good mood. He can't believe how improved the roads are; the Chinese have been busy. When Kazz was here 30 years ago the roads were barely passable. Back then it took him a week to cover the distance we have in our three days of travel.

We cross the great Tibetan plateau, often called the roof of the world. It feels like we are on another planet. It is arid and wind swept, and since we are above the tree line there are only occasional tussocks of grass. Dorji explains that geologically, Tibet is an ancient seabed. About 50 million years ago, the Indian subcontinent slid north and collided with Eurasia. As it slammed into what is now China, the floor of the Tethys Ocean, which had separated the two landmasses, was lifted, forming Tibet with the Himalaya and Karakoram mountain ranges. This is the origin of the prized Himalayan pink sea salt and the marine fossils sometimes found on the surface of the high plateau.

Dorji talks proudly about ancient Tibetan history, but he is understandably cautious when it comes to present-day subjects. Tibet may be the inspiration for the mythical, earthly paradise Shangri-La, but it is also a country of conflict. The Chinese have firmly controlled Tibet since the 1950s, destroying thousands of monasteries and brutally suppressing opposition. Tibetans see it as an illegal occupation; the Chinese see it as liberation from a corrupt theocracy and nobility. Dorji acknowledges progressive improvements like roads, new homes, and a power infrastructure, and even goes so far as to credit the current Chinese governor with finally acknowledging Tibetan customs and ways of life. But he tells us all this as if he were reading from a script. He has a family to support and the government carefully monitors the lucrative tourist industry, which he is a part of. Only when it comes to the Dali Lama does Dorji show any disregard for what the Chinese rulers think. His greatest dream is one day to meet the exiled spiritual leader of the Tibetan people.

"What is the future of Tibet?" I ask.

Dorji shrugs, "The Chinese are here to stay. Even the Dalai Lama says that. We just have to learn to live together. It's our karma."

At that moment I ask Sitar our driver to stop so I can photograph the stunning landscape and pee. As I jump out of the car and aim my lens I mumble to myself, "And I thought what I am going through is difficult..."

After three days of determined driving on mostly paved, newly built roads, we finally arrive at Lake Manasarovar at the foot of Mt. Kailash. Tomorrow we'll drive the short distance to Tarchen, the gateway for the pilgrimage. We are now on truly hallowed grounds. Mt.

Kailash is just to the north, but it is shrouded in clouds. At 4,590 meters (15,060 ft), Lake Manasarovar is the highest large fresh-water lake in the world. Pilgrims from all over the world venerate it. It is the *yin* to Mt. Kailash's *yang*, a still body of water to the pulsating energy of the dramatic mountain.

Our lodging is located below the Chiu Gompa monastery. It is already filled with pilgrims who have been here for the last few days. After we move our bags from the Toyota Land Cruiser to our simple guesthouse room we head to the lake. I leave behind the proxies for my dead grandparents and my parents' ashes, and only carry my camera and a small fanny pack.

We walk slowly along the edge, taking the most we can from the thin air, past small groups of Hindu pilgrims praying and splashing water from the holy lake on themselves. A dip in its deep emerald-green waters absolves them of all sins, and a ritual circumnavigation of its 92-kilometer shoreline, like a trip around Mt. Kailash, insures the walker a place in heaven.

Flocks of black-headed gulls fill the sky, and colonies of coots and terns nest near the shore. The birds are protected, and so are oblivious as I come close and snap one photo after another. Neither boats nor fishing are allowed on the lake.

Following the shoreline for about 20 minutes, we come to a jumble of rocks marked by tattered prayer flags; a path leads up the side of the cliff to a small opening overlooking the lake. We scramble up. There is just enough room for the two of us to sit in the cave with our backs against the rock. It is easy to imagine other pilgrims sitting here day after day, night after night, year after year, considering their lives and contemplating the universe. I no longer feel so alone on my quest to make things right. Along with Kazz, I sense countless others who have come before me, and others who will follow.

A distant dark cloud drops rain onto the surface of the lake.

Lake Manasarovar.

It suddenly occurs to me I am witnessing both the birth and death of the rivers that empty out of Lake Manasarovar. In a flash of insight I see how all rivers, both metaphorical and real, represent a never-ending cycle. The clouds feed the lake with water, the essence of life. The lake feeds the river, and the river ends up at the sea, only to be transformed into clouds once again. Thinking this way doesn't change the fact that my brother left a stain on our family river, but it does inherently make what he did a part of a larger whole. When I share my thoughts with Kazz he nods and smiles.

As the rain reaches the shoreline Kazz and I scrabble down the cliff, pull our hoods over our heads, and walk quickly back to camp, passing the Indian pilgrims who are sitting calmly and chanting in the now drenching downpour. Back at our room, Dorji tells us a 50-year-old Indian woman from Bangalore died during the night from altitude sickness. He says this makes 11 people who have died in the last few weeks. He wants to know how we feel; we are his responsibility. I can see he is relieved to hear we feel fine.

78

We are in Tarchen, the starting point for our walk around the mountain. I still haven't seen Mt. Kailash; it remains hidden behind a heavy layer of clouds. Everywhere we go in town we see heaps of garbage spilling onto the muddy, unpaved streets. As I step around the piles of filth I find it hard to believe we are really in the shadow of one of the most sacred places on earth.

Just after noon, the clouds hiding the peak finally blow away. The photos I've seen of the mountain don't do it justice. It's not like any of the other mountains in the Himalaya and Kunlun ranges. It looks more like a precious jewel or a pyramid than a mountain and its sharply cut sides of rock and snow-covered peak shimmer against the bright blue sky. In the mountain's radiance the heaps of garbage that bothered me so much have disappeared.

That night at a run-down café off the main street, dinner is barely edible. We leave most of our dish of chicken bones swimming in greasy noodles untouched. In our hostel room we prepare a package of freeze-dried food from REI that Rebecca insisted I bring. As we eat I ask Kazz if he remembers the meal we had at my parents' home in Livermore a few days before Rebecca's and my wedding.

"I remember your father wanted you and Rebecca to sleep in the bomb shelter on your wedding night," he replies after a few moments. "He fixed it up for you."

"I forgot all about that," I say. "I outgrew the need for the bomb shelter long ago."

Kazz reaches for a thermos full of hot tea and pours himself a cup.

"The meal?" I continue. "My father put a perfectly good pot roast, potatoes, and carrots in a blender. He served us baby food! You were the only one who ate it. Remember now?"

"It was good," Kazz says, finishing off the last of his tea. "Better than we get here!" And with that we both laugh so hard our sides ache and we slip into bed. Before falling into a sound and satisfying sleep, I say softly to Kazz and the darkness, "My father always tried his best to be there for me. I really miss him."

Our trek around the mountain begins before dawn. The full moon is low on the horizon and it casts a dim light over the bleak landscape as we walk from our hotel through Tarchen to the trailhead. We are followed by a pack of feral dogs and Dorji is nervous. At night these dogs are vicious and fearless. He throws rocks to keep them away. We hit the main trail just as the sky turns pink. Just ahead of us is a woman with a small child strapped to her back . She wears a mask to protect her face and skin from the harsh, dry winds.

It is Kazz's 61st birthday and we are in good spirits. As we walk I sing "Happy Birthday" to him. He is embarrassed, but I keep singing anyway. We are now the same age. Two teen-age boys hired by Dorji carry our bags. Kazz has moved his things, including his sacred objects, to a duffle bag and agreed to leave his suitcase behind at the guesthouse. The boys run quickly ahead and I have to ask the one carrying the bag with my extra lenses not to get too far ahead. He is also carrying my drinking water and rain gear. We don't need the gear now but the weather is unpredictable. Sure enough, it is soon pouring down rain.

A natural path circles around the mountain through the rock and shale. We walk around this perimeter to honor and respect the mountain, and also to gather merit and good fortune. There is no reward for conquering the summit and we have no desire to even try. Due to its nearly vertical incline and also because the Tibetans don't allow it, Mt. Kailash has never been scaled by anyone, even though it is "only" 6,638 meters (21,778 feet), compared to Mt. Everest's 8,848 meters (29,029 feet). The Tibetan word for pilgrimage is *neykhor*, which means to circle around a sacred place. The Buddhists call the walk a *kora*, and the Hindus call it a *parikrama*. I call it tying up loose ends.

In front of us now is the Tarboche flagpole, the site of the Saga Dawa Festival, which officially opens the pilgrimage season in the spring. After a short gain of altitude we drop down into the Lha Chu Valley, its flat, gravelly bottom boxed in by huge sculpted granite rock formations, broken crags, and scree-covered slopes.

Running parallel to our path is the swiftly flowing Lha Chu River, a tributary of the mighty Brahmaputra River, which eventually empties into the Bay of Bengal. For a while I walk alongside Harry, a 13-year-old boy from Beijing who is here with his family. I ask him what he wants to be when he grows up. Without hesitation, he says a professor. I ask him why and he says that way he won't have to work too hard. I laugh and give him thumbs up.

Around 5:00 p.m. we cross a bridge over the Lha Chu River and trudge wearily upwards toward the Dira-puk monastery. Near the monastery is a newly built guesthouse, but the receptionist tells us it is full. Dorji, who seems to know everyone everywhere we go, finds the manager and in a few minutes we are offered a comfortable three-person room with plaster walls and a stunning view of Mt. Kailash, now only partially obscured by clouds. Our two young helpers disappear to a communal sleeping room where they join other young Tibetans assisting foreigners. From their appearances the next morning, it is a fun night without much sleep.

We are exhausted but our day is not over. This is the day Kazz has planned and dreamed about for years. He carries with him two heavy stones from Japan, hollowed out and filled with holy objects. One of them contains the final

Mt. Kailash

piece of the Sword of Heaven, an ancient Shinto artifact that was the centerpiece of a peace project started over 40 years before and involving many people. I finished my part of the project years ago, but Kazz isn't done yet. The other stone is filled with objects wholly of Kazz's choice. It is his personal offering to the mountain, and a summation of his life. Dorji looks surprised when we tell him we are going out to explore. We have hiked 21 kilometers and climbed 300 meters. He says we should stay and rest. He reminds us tomorrow's trek is the most difficult of all: 25 kilometers including the formidable climb to the Dolma La pass.

As we leave the guesthouse and cross back over the river, we are suddenly pummeled with pea-sized hail accompanied by huge explosions of thunder. The wind whips the hail forcibly against my poncho and my face. I think we should turn back.

"It's a good omen," Kazz says to my concern. "The storm chases away the bad spirits and cleans our mind and bodies."

"You are soaking wet and nearly blown off the trail and you are happy?" I grumble.

"Of course!" answers Kazz enthusiastically. "Very happy."

We follow a loud stream fed by melting snow and rain tumbling down from the mountain. Periodically, the weather breaks and we see glimpses of the impressive peak in front of us. Kazz walks silently several meters ahead of me, weaving past giant boulders in our path. By now I am lightheaded and between gasps for air I chat with the mountain as if it were an old friend. I tell it how beautiful it is and how lucky I am to be here. When the mountain disappears behind the clouds, I ask it not to be shy and please come back. I consider bringing up my brother Hans and talking about what he did and perhaps holding my ancestor meeting here; I have everything I need for the meeting with me. But even though I am mildly delirious I have enough sense to know that this is

Kazz's time and mine will have to come later.

About an hour later, around 7:00 p.m., we stop at the spot where the mountain abruptly shoots up to the sky. We stop at a large, angular boulder and Kazz pulls a collapsible shovel from his backpack. He then sits and digs a large opening underneath the rock. I stand back a few meters and videotape him scraping at the hard earth. When he is finished he slips into the white jacket he bought in Kathmandu, leaving a purple woven cap on his head to protect it from the freezing wind.

Kazz begins the Shinto placing ritual by clapping his hands together two times, followed by a series of chants, more claps, and more chants. He repeatedly calls out the name *Amaterasu*, the Sun Goddess and the highest deity in the Shinto pantheon. He prays to the other pieces of the Sword of Heaven placed around the globe, calling on the *kamis* to protect the earth from bad spirits. He goes on like this for about 15 minutes and by the time he finishes burying the sacred objects under the rock it is nearly dark. This is Kazz's show and now I am the one watching *his* back. We hurry back down the side of the mountain to our room.

Dorji is relived to see us. I'm sure the last thing he wants to do is organize an emergency airlift for two old fools who didn't listen to him.

The second day of our trip around the mountain, the most difficult of them all, starts with a quick breakfast of *gjetost*, a brown goat cheese I carried from Norway, and whole wheat bread we bought at the Pumpernickel café in

Kathmandu. Some horses and riders are already in front of us, moving quickly, but most of the other pilgrims are behind us.

As we trudge up the rocky trail and gain altitude it becomes increasingly hard to breathe. My legs feel heavy and I am unsteady. A light rain and more hail make the trail especially slippery. We still have several hundred meters to go to the pass, which is 5630 meters (18,500 feet) high. I've never walked at this altitude before and I think of the Indian woman who died a few days earlier of altitude sickness. I've successfully climbed Mt. Shasta in northern California several times, but it is only 4,322 meters (14,179 feet) and I did it when I was much younger, before doctors placed two stents in my heart and stitched up my stomach.

On the side of the trail we see empty cans of heavily caffeinated Red Bull, a popular energy drink among trekkers. I power up on a Kvikk Lunsj, a Norwegian chocolate-covered wafer bar. I also force myself to drink water even when I don't feel thirsty. Like other men on the trail, I pee just to the side of the trail with minimal consideration for privacy. Women go an extra meter or so off the trail to do their business.

Before long we see Indian pilgrims who have given up and are returning on horses to the lower elevations. They have a pained, defeated look on their faces. Their parikrama has been cut short.

"They think they have failed," Kazz says to me when I ask. "But making it this far is a success."

Many Tibetans are also coming down from the pass toward us, but they have not turned back; they are the Bon, worshipers of the native religion of Tibet. While the Buddhist and Hindus walk clockwise, the Bons circumnavigate the mountain counterclockwise. When they pass us on the trail they are invariably cheerful, glowing with an otherworldly happiness. They are spry and full of energy. All of them seem at home here on the trail, surrounded by rocks and rivers and clouds and mountains. I smile when they pass and they smile back and call out *tashidele*, or good luck, a traditional Tibetan greeting.

"Bon and Shintoism both worship nature and ancestors and believe spirits dwell in the land," explains Kazz as we trudge breathlessly up the hill. "They both contain the bedrock other religions stand on."

Kazz and I continue, counting out a few steps then stopping to rest. I take photos of the climbers in front of me and the ones behind me. Although I am tired, my thinking has become sharp and clear, like the thin air around me.

Once again, I find myself obsessing about garbage. Besides the cans of Red Bull, there are cans of Coke and empty plastic bottles and wrappers, and even human excrement. I complain to Kazz, who is leaning against a boulder resting. "You haven't traveled much in this part of Asia, have you?" he says.

Finally, when we are within sight of the pass, I realize once again I have tuned out the good things and prioritized the bad. I can choose what to focus on. I see garbage when I could be appreciating the beauty that surrounds me. I imagine my wise daughter Miranda telling me to *perspectify*, a word she invented and uses when she wants me to step back and look at the bigger picture. With this thought, the garbage doesn't go away but I see it in a different light.

At the Dolma La pass, the trail is surrounded by streams of colorful prayer flags partially covered in snow. We stop for a short rest. I would like to spend more time savoring our accomplishment but the air is too thin and I know we still have a long way to go. After drinking from our water bottles and taking a few photos we quickly start our descent. The hail has turned to cold rain and the muddy path on this side of the pass is even more slippery and dangerous. I use two walking

A Bon pilgrim.

sticks for added stability. At one point, we turn a corner and see a Tibetan man and woman crawling toward us on their hands and knees through the mud. They are wearing plastic sandals on their hands to protect them from the rocky ground. As we get closer they rise to their knees, clasp their hands together and pray. Then they prostrate themselves back on the trail and start crawling forward again. Kazz explains to me that these pilgrims, and others like them, get special spiritual dispensation for circling the mountain in this grueling way. The physical toll is enormous and it can take weeks to complete. I will be safely back in Norway long before they are finished.

Finally we make it to the Lham Chu valley. The worst is behind us. It is still several hours until we reach the Zutul-puk monastery where we will overnight, but the valley floor is mostly level and as long as we walk slow it is easy going. When we arrive, it is almost dark and I am dead tired but still very much alive.

At 3:30 in the morning I wake up coughing in a room filled with thick hazy smoke. Across the dark room I see Bon pilgrims smoking and sipping yak butter tea and preparing for an early start. The yak-dung stove in the middle of the communal room is burning brightly and leaks smoke profusely. For the moment, I am grateful the extreme altitude has dulled my sense of smell. Two young children sit on the edge of my sleeping bag and I point my camera phone at them. At first they protest, then they smile. Remarkably, I have cell phone coverage here in the high mountains of Tibet and I post the photo on Facebook.

Rebecca has sent me several text messages assuring me

everything is fine with her and the girls. It is good they are not with me. I can imagine my daughter's faces if they faced an open pit toilet or were served stewed yak meat, or had to sleep on a flea-infested mattress, as I am doing right now. Someday they might appreciate this kind of adventure, but not now, as hard-to-please teenagers.

The third and final day is the easiest of all, even though I hardly slept the night before and yesterday was so demanding. We walk slowly but we are still at the trail's end before noon. Sitar, our Tibetan driver, is at the end of the trail with our Toyota. While we walked he visited his sister, who lives and works nearby. We tip our young helpers generously and causally say goodbye, as if walking around the mountain was something we do all the time.

There are no cheering crowds waiting for us, no medals or badges of honor. Just a few years ago when I was lying in the ER I would never have imagined doing what I have just done. I have proved I am physically fit, but what else have I accomplished?

I am sitting on the bank of the shallow Horchu River, a few hundred meters from where it meets Lake Manasarovar. It rained all night and I woke up soaking wet under a leaky tin roof, but now the sun is bright and the sky is mostly clear except for a dark band of clouds on the horizon. I can see Mt. Kailash reflected on the surface of the river. A gentle wind occasionally disturbs the surface and ripples partially distort my view of the majestic peak. Kazz is by my side. We walked here together through swampy grassland from our lodging about a kilometer away. There is no one else in sight. Later today we start the long journey

The Dzong-chu River is on the right,

our trail on the left.

back to Kathmandu. I have chosen the end of our time in this holy place to hold another family meeting, now that we have successfully circumnavigated Mt. Kailash.

Kazz knows it didn't go well back in San Francisco the first time. Now he will provide a backdrop of traditional Shinto chanting and praying. More than anything, he is my wingman, like I was for him, here to lend moral support and help make this meeting a success.

As I arrange my parents' ashes and the objects representing my ancestors in front of me, I hear Kazz clap his hands two times. As he begins a melodic chant I call the family meeting to order. I immediately sense the presence of my four grandparents, as well as my mother and my father. In my mind each of my relatives is distinct from the other, but my image of them blurs and I see them as a single entity.

I welcome everyone here to this high mountain river in Tibet and I get the feeling everyone, like me, is in awe of the sacred surroundings. It is a long way from Grand Rapids, Michigan, where my mother and her parents lived, and where my grandfather is buried in the veteran's cemetery. It is a long way from Ulefoss, where my father and his parents are from. Only my father has been even close to this part of the world, docking briefly in Bombay, 1,500 kilometers to the south.

No one is surprised by my call, and unlike my first family meeting, I feel surrounded by a warm, comforting embrace, complete with the positive affirmation I have been looking for. My ancestors applaud my journey to Tibet. The trail around the mountain, they say, is like a river with no end. By walking it I have symbolically made whole what was broken and atoned for my brother's crime, a crime I have always felt partially responsible for. They say it may take a while to sink in, but I have done the best I can. Atonement, literally at oneness, will eventually lead me to peace of mind.

The Horchu River and my parents' ashes.

Up to this moment my father has not been a particularly strong presence, but now he makes it clear that no one in the family, especially him, is angry with Hans for what he did. He is just sad and wishes it could have been otherwise. He is satisfied Hans is in good hands and well taken care of, and hopes he will make the most of what is left of his life.

My family meeting doesn't last long. Kazz finishes chanting and sits quietly by the river. I hear my ancestors, speaking as one voice, say it is time for me to move on, to put what happened behind me—to look beyond the garbage in my life—and appreciate all the good things that remain. I toss the golf ball, the fishing lure (at our first meeting it was my grandfather's pipe), the bath salts, the flower, and finally my parents' ashes into the stream. The ashes join together in a way my parents never could when they were alive.

I look up and see Mt. Kailash towering majestically in the distance. I ask myself whether I have really done what I started out to do. Have I cleaned the family river? Have I restored the balance? I want to say yes, but I know the answer will come later, not from me, not from my ancestors, but from my children and their children and their children's children. I can say this: At this moment I feel a weight has lifted from my shoulders and I no longer feel burdened by my father's death, or my brother's act. I am free.

As I get up to follow Kazz back to our lodging I imagine my mother's voice and a satisfied look on her face. I hear her say nearly the same words she used when she woke from a coma, a short time before she died. Her words are no longer posed as a question. They are an answer.

"*This* is the end of the book."

She is right. Being here, doing what I have just done, is the perfect ending to my long struggle. Now it is time to go home.

POSTSCRIPT

Turn your face to the sun
and the shadows fall behind you.

—*Maori Proverb*

I have navigated the river I call my life through rapids and falls, through twists and turns, through the waters of madness, patricide, and atonement. It is eleven years since my father's death. I am in San Francisco working at the same desk where this story began. The river has changed course, and so have I.

In 2013 we lost my aunt Nøve to cancer, but not before she outlived her doctor's predictions and gifted us with several bonus years. Even though Norway will never be the same without her, we still summer at our home in Ulefoss and in the future, after the girls finish school, Rebecca and I hope to extend our time there. Both our lovely daughters are teenagers now. God help us through these difficult years!

Hans is at Gladman and his legal case is still in limbo and will probably remain so for the foreseeable future. About once a month, ever since Mom's memorial, my brother Erik and I take Hans out to lunch at a Mexican restaurant a few blocks from the mental health rehabilitation center. We share old memories and afterwards, while Hans leans back in his chair with a faraway look on his face Erik and I argue good-naturedly about whose turn it is to pay the bill.

All rivers end up at the sea. All stories come to an end. I am done with this story but I will never be done with the river in my backyard.

My family and me in 2008.

Acknowledgements

The writing and production of this book took seven years and along the way many people helped. I would like to thank Sarah Lazin, Jay Schaefer, Sean Webby, Catherine Dombrose, Perry Garfinkel, Pauline Frommer, David Elliot Cohen, Fred Soloway, Sandra McHenry, Debra Neuenschwander Millar, Mary Becker, Monica Suder, Julie Christensen, Jon Anders Halvorsen, Lauren Cuthburt, Katharina Reschke, Angela Robinson, Jean Carpenter, Eric and Margrete Geurts-Lakin, and Bryon MacWilliams who read the manuscript (sometimes several versions!) and provided valuable feedback and advice. A special thanks to Phil Cousineau who helped keep me on track at some especially dark moments.

Often all I needed was a receptive ear and a perceptive comment and for that I would like to thank Leonard Koren, Nathan Benn, Rebecca Abrams, Dan Brodnitz, V. Vale, Hans Peter Brøndmo, Anne Lise Flavik, Bruce Yelaska, Cheryl Parker, Rudy Burger, Tom Mogensen, Eran Steinberg, Laena Wilder, Tore and Linda Waal Halvorsen, Richard Morgenstein, Fanny Renoir, Martin Unger, Erling Maartmann-Moe, David Sheff, Michael Lester, Leo Laporte, Daniel Ben-Horin, Sara Tucker, Peter Krogh, Gro Viberto, Bitsy Taggart Fitzsimmons, Bjørn G. Halvorsen, Halvor K. Halvorsen, Arvid Hoegvoll, Atle Grotmol, Bill and Sioux Atkinson, Bruce Dale, Don George, Jan Odinsen, Liz Skardal, Leif Heisholt, Greg Moga, Ryan Rosenberg, Ben and Wilma Zweerts, Andrew Tarnowka, Dennis Hearne, Bonnie Bills, Monica Lee, Jonathan Rapp, Steven Axelrod, Billy Robinson, Shauna Woods, Peter and Zuzana Willits, Maggie Hallahan, Jo Beaton, Bob Steinberg, Liz Lufkin, Tony Carey, Svein Narum, Julie Grahame, Chris Mittelstaedt, Pia Hinckle, Wendy Burger, Luis Delgado, Ellen Deitch, Tim Grey, David Willey, Kate Kelly, Bernard Ohanian, Janelle Balnicke, Alexis Gerard, Wolfgang Ettlich, Judy Golden, Greg Mitchell, Micha Peled, Michael Shapiro, and Dave Drum.

While writing this book I participated in Rebecca Walker's *The Art of Memoir* workshop. Rebecca is a brilliant writer and a gifted teacher who helped guide me in the right direction. Thanks also to my other workshop participants Renee Ferguson, Beverly Bond, Petrina Khashoggi, Dolores Johnson, and Quddus Philippe.

Thank you Isabel Allende for all you have done for me and the world. You inspire us all.

The process of producing this book was challenging. Helping me with all the moving parts was: Tim Peek, Pete Vilotti, Rebecca Morgen, Sarah Hillesheim, Peter Truskier, Bill Petrocelli, Sam Barry, Harold and Phyllis Davis, James Levin, Maureen Wheeler, Linda Watanabe McFerrin, and Mark Brokering.

Finally I want to thank Lori Barra for her steadfast support, encouragement, friendship, and beautiful book design, my daughters Miranda and Ana who often contributed words of uncanny wisdom, and my wife, Rebecca Taggart without whom this book would not have been even remotely possible.

CPSIA information can be obtained
at www.ICGtesting.com
Printed in the USA
BVHW021313230321
603267BV00018B/411